INTIMACY FROM THE INSIDE OUT

Couples in distress enter therapy holding two goals that they now experience as mutually exclusive: to feel loved and to feel understood. Toni Herbine-Blank's powerful new brand of couple therapy, Intimacy from the Inside Out (IFIO), offers a comprehensive conceptual map for achieving both goals. In a tour de force of elegant case illustrations wrapped around clear instruction, this book shows the IFIO therapist working with the natural subdivisions – or parts – of the human mind in a dyad, guiding and supporting couples to understand how they project childhood injury into current relationships and then, feeling threatened, frustrated and angry, lose track of their underlying needs to feel safe, connected and loved. With a focus on generating internal attachment stability to sustain each partner through the moments when the other is unavailable, couples in IFIO therapy reconnect with their essential needs, change their conversations and learn to make requests that invite rather than threaten in order to get those needs met.

Toni Herbine-Blank, MS, RN, Cs-P, is a senior trainer for the Center for Self-Leadership and the sole developer of Intimacy from the Inside Out (IFIO). She runs trainings, retreats and workshops on both methods nationally and internationally and has a private psychotherapy practice in Durango, Colorado. For more information: toniherbineblank.com.

Donna M. Kerpelman, JD, MS, has been immersed in Internal Family Systems (IFS) for more than ten years as a student, teacher and therapist. She has organized and facilitated several IFIO retreats for couples in addition to assisting in IFIO trainings for couple therapists. She also brings her knowledge of IFS and relationships to the legal world where she represents children with lead poisoning.

Martha Sweezy, PhD, has a therapy and consultation practice in Northampton, Massachusetts. She is a clinical supervisor at Cambridge Health Alliance, a Lecturer in Psychiatry at Harvard Medical School, an occasional helper at IFS trainings, and co-leads workshops on the topic of shame. She is author of several articles on IFS, and co-editor, with Ellen Ziskind, of two volumes on IFS: *Innovations and Elaborations on Internal Family Systems Therapy* and *Internal Family Systems Therapy: New Dimensions.* For more information: marthasweezy.com.

INTIMACY FROM THE INSIDE OUT

Courage and Compassion in Couple Therapy

*Toni Herbine-Blank,
Donna M. Kerpelman and
Martha Sweezy*

NEW YORK AND LONDON

First published 2016
by Routledge
711 Third Avenue, New York, NY 10017

and by Routledge
2 Park Square, Milton Park, Abingdon, Oxon OX14 4RN

Routledge is an imprint of the Taylor & Francis Group, an informa business

Library of Congress Cataloging-in-Publication Data
Herbine-Blank, Toni.
Intimacy from the inside out : courage and compassion in couple therapy / authored by Toni Herbine-Blank, Donna M. Kerpelman, Martha Sweezy.
  pages cm
  Includes bibliographical references and index.
  1. Couples therapy. 2. Intimacy. 3. Interpersonal conflict. I. Kerpelman, Donna M. II. Sweezy, Martha. III. Title.
  RC488.5.H477 2016
  616.89'1562–dc23   2015006414

ISBN: 978-0-415-70824-1 (hbk)
ISBN: 978-0-415-70825-8 (pbk)
ISBN: 978-1-315-88614-5 (ebk)

Typeset in Baskerville
by Wearset Ltd, Boldon, Tyne and Wear

Toni Herbine-Blank
To all beings who courageously choose the sometimes arduous path of conscious, open hearted relationships. And to Jordan Blank, my husband, who is on this path with me and continually inspires me to walk my talk.

Donna M. Kerpelman
To Saul, my love and my light.
And to my Mom and Dad, whose enduring love continues to inspire me.

Martha Sweezy
To my parents, Nancy & Paul Sweezy, who time and again chose courage and clarity.

CONTENTS

Foreword by Richard Schwartz   ix
Acknowledgments   xi

Introduction   1

PHASE 1
Beginning   9

1 The Origins of Intimacy from the Inside Out
  Therapy   11

2 Getting to Know the Couple and Introducing the
  Model   21

PHASE 2
The Flow and Eddies of the Middle   37

3 Tracking Cycles   39

4 Courageous Communication   50

5 Individual Work   73

6 Countertransference in Couple Therapy   85

7 Negotiating Needs   95

8 You, Me, We? Negotiating Corresponding Needs that
  Conflict   106

9 Shaming and Feeling Shamed in Couple Therapy   116

10 Deepening Experiential Work   131

11 What Makes a Difficult Case Difficult?   145

PHASE 3
Ending   155

12 Repairing Relationship Rupture   157

Appendix 1: Unblending   176
Appendix 2: Unburdening   178
Glossary   179
References   183
Index   186

FOREWORD

One of the most gratifying things for someone who devotes his life to the creation of a modality of psychotherapy is to have it expanded, improved upon and beautifully applied to a specific population by a person of immense talent. I am very grateful to Toni Herbine-Blank (with help from Donna M. Kerpelman and Martha Sweezy) for giving me this experience. This book is a wonderful contribution not only to the growing literature on IFS but to the whole field of couple therapy.

The book takes a topic of immense complexity – how the two internal systems of a couple collide with each other to produce the rigid patterns that drive them toward dissolution – and in simple, clear language makes it understandable. Along the way, it offers time-tested techniques for helping each partner drop their weapons, focus inside and speak to each other from a different place – the Self. When couples are able to do this, each partner invariably develops new insight and also discovers that speaking from the Self on behalf of (rather than from) both protective and vulnerable parts produces an entirely different response from the partner. In IFS we have the expression "Self heals" and that is true for external relationships as well as internal ones. The good news is that the healing Self is just beneath the surface of each partner's protectors. Toni offers needed wisdom to therapists who seek to create safety and help the couple access the Self. When they do, their relationship will heal itself.

This book has great strengths. First, not only does it explain IFS and IFIO concepts clearly as they apply to couples, it also offers vivid examples throughout, with long, engaging passages of dialogue which bring Toni's concepts and techniques to life by putting the reader in her shoes.

Second, the topic of therapist parts is well covered. Working with couples inevitably triggers all kinds of therapist parts and once that happens the therapy is doomed unless the therapist is able to recognize that s/he is triggered and return to Self-leadership. Between Toni's disclosure of her process during sessions and the book's discussions about common triggers for therapists, this important topic is covered thoughtfully and thoroughly throughout the book. Indeed, her commentary consistently teaches the reader how to help the partners do a U-turn to find and heal the parts who are frozen in the childhood scenes that fuel their conflict.

In summary, this book builds on the framework I developed for working with couples, not only translating that material for therapists but also adding the important concepts and methods of IFIO that are not in my book. The case dialogue is so well written that I found myself choking up at times in recognition of the patterns described and the courage it took for partners to finally express their vulnerability.

Last, this book showcases Toni's development as a therapist, teacher and theorist. When I first got to know her fifteen years ago, I saw this potential – her charisma, special presence, articulateness and sensitivity. This work is a tribute to her personal growth, which allows her Self to shine and has made her a leader in the IFS community. If there is justice in the world, Toni will be a major figure in the field of couple therapy. I'm delighted that IFS travels with the IFIO banner into that field.

Richard Schwartz
Boston, MA
December 1, 2014

ACKNOWLEDGMENTS

Toni Herbine-Blank:
My deep appreciation goes to my co-authors Donna M. Kerpelman and Martha Sweezy. Donna, who spent the good portion of a year transcribing lectures, writing and editing the first draft of this book, has been a champion of IFIO since its inception in 1999. I am deeply grateful for her steadfast support, her passion for the model and her friendship. Martha, who began encouraging me to write about multiplicity in couple therapy years ago, has edited and rewritten that first draft with great care and respect, all the while inspiring me to be ever more creative in clarifying my ideas. Martha's skill and experience have been a major gift in my life as well as in writing this book. She continues to encourage me to empower myself, think outside the box and be fearless about expanding the model. I am thankful for her expertise, enthusiasm and friendship.

I give special thanks and appreciation to Dick Schwartz, my friend and mentor. I cannot thank him enough for trusting me and encouraging me to take this aspect of his model and make it my own. His support is meaningful beyond words.

There would be no clinical material except for the brave couples who put themselves in therapy with the wish to transform their relationships. The model itself is derived from these courageous people. They have been my teachers and mentors.

In addition, many people have supported and encouraged me over the years, some of whom travel the country to staff IFIO trainings continually and tirelessly. These dedicated colleagues do research, brainstorm, teach, mentor others and use the model in their therapy practice with vigor and enthusiasm. I give special thanks to my dedicated staff, Ann Drouilhet, Kate Lingren, Robin Warsh, Judi Zoldan, and to my IFIO trainers, past and present, Michele Bograd, Pamela Geib, Sarah Stewart and Nancy Wonder for their particular contributions. And thanks to everyone who read the manuscript and gave us crucial feedback to help this manuscript evolve.

I am also moved to mention the many people whose development of and writings about couple therapy have inspired me. Most important is my Imago trainer and mentor Sunny Schulkin, who taught me to be courageous and open hearted regardless of what model I was using and to be fearlessly present and hold my seat no matter what the circumstance.

For my thoughts about apology, forgiveness and self-forgiveness I am indebted to Buddhist philosophy, Janis Abrams Springs on repair and forgiveness, and Richard Schwartz on *Self and parts* in regard to apology.

Last, I offer my deepest gratitude to my family and close friends who reside far from the world of IFIO and have cheered me on, held my hand, offered solace, helped with editing and on and on. I give special thanks to my mother and father, Deetsie and Fritz Herbine, and my sister and brother-in-law, Kate and Joel Feldman. And most important I give thanks to my husband, Jordan, who is my greatest champion in all endeavors, no matter how small or large.

Donna M. Kerpelman:
Toni Herbine-Blank is one of those rare teachers who lights up the room with her enthusiasm, intelligence, humility and genuine desire to connect with her audience. She is a brilliant psychotherapist and trainer and it has been my great privilege to work with her in many venues. I am honored to have had the opportunity to help put her important work into words so that more people will have access to all that she has dedicated her life to understanding and sharing. Many

thanks to Martha Sweezy, a gifted writer and editor, for joining us in this endeavor.

Martha Sweezy:
Toni was my first teacher in an IFS training, after which I made a point of taking several more with her. I want to offer a virtual bow here to her extraordinary gifts and skill as a teacher, thinker and clinician. And I thank both Toni and Donna for the opportunity to participate in writing this book.

INTRODUCTION

My career in couple therapy began following graduate school in the early 1990s. A few years later, when I felt a need to help the individuals who were in couple therapy with me do their own deep intrapsychic work, a dear friend introduced me to Internal Family Systems therapy (IFS), an approach to working with individuals and families that Richard Schwartz (1995) developed in the 1980s and later expanded to include couples, as he describes in his book *You're the One You've Been Waiting For* (2008). Although confused by his model at first, I could also see the power and beauty of his work. His confidence in the resilience of his clients, his skill, respect and patience were so inspiring that I signed on to learn more and had the good fortune to be mentored and trained by Schwartz for several years before becoming an IFS trainer myself in 2006.

As a trainer I first taught the basics of using the IFS model with individuals but eventually I turned to teaching about couple therapy as well. Here I found that I had more to say than I could fit into the allotted training hours. Since relational work had long been my interest and passion, I spent the next few years developing a methodology of couple therapy based primarily on IFS but also combined with what I knew from years of previous training and countless clinical hours with couples. I taught the first version of Intimacy from the Inside Out© (IFIO) to a group of advanced IFS practitioners in Boston, Massachusetts in 2009. Since then, IFIO has been an exciting work in progress for me. My co-authors and I wrote this book as a road map for therapists who wish to learn and apply my curriculum.

The Blueprint for IFIO

IFIO couple therapy involves the dialectic between planning for the universals that we can predict and responding skillfully to everything else. We can predict, for example, that people long to feel safe, to love and be loved. And we can predict that they will have injured parts who were exiled in any number of ways by protective parts, whose *protection*, needed as it once was, has become an integral part of the problem. We can also predict that we will need to gain the cooperation of a client's protectors in order to be effective in treatment. We cover many other predictable aspects of the mind and behavior in the chapters that follow.

In contrast, there is a big range of content issues (like an affair) or behavioral interactions in the room (like rage) that can arise with any couple but which remain unpredictable because they do not occur with everyone. These are more likely to blindside the therapist. In IFIO, our goal is to unblend from our own protectors so that no matter what is happening, we can respond to the couple spontaneously, from the heart, able to draw on skills (from inner wisdom, life experience and training) but remain unattached to ideas about how things ought to go.

The Therapist's Essential Dialectic: Being Prepared and Being Self-led

On one side of this blueprint we have the skill of being prepared, which, as mentioned, involves knowing and understanding that which is universal and predictable: the multiple structure of the mind and how it functions, which involves *parts* (as Schwartz dubbed these phenomena) and an undamaged core *Self* (Schwartz, 1995). This Self (which everyone has) channels the emotions necessary for psychic balance, including curiosity and compassion, and exhibits remarkable emotional stability and wisdom. But when a person is shamed, protective parts step in. Their protective strategies can be life saving in the short run, but will recapitulate the original injury, inside and out, in the long run. All of this we know.

On the other side of the blueprint for IFIO therapists, we have the skill of being *Self-led* (Schwartz, 1995) and handling the unpredictable. Being Self-led involves being in good relationship to your parts so that you can separate from them or *unblend* (Schwartz, 1995) and be present with whatever occurs, applying Self-energy and your intuitive knowledge of the right tool for the moment. Keeping this dialectic between the predictable and the unpredictable in mind, we take you through three phases of treatment in this book: the beginning, middle and end.

The Three Phases of Treatment

The beginning, Phase 1, is covered in Chapter 2, which describes what to look for as you get to know the couple, and how to introduce the IFIO model.

The middle, Phase 2, covers the majority of this therapy. To capture the forward pull exerted by the couple's longing to reconnect along with the inevitable circling of stony spots that constitutes therapy we named Phase 2 *The Flow and Eddies of the Middle*. Our process is non-linear. We repeat new learning that contradicts the couple's old and cherished ideas about how to be safe, we challenge their entrenched protectors kindly, and we help them to heal old wounds. Of necessity we move back and forth between what we know – the predictable – and what comes up with this particular couple, in this moment – the unpredictable. To handle the latter, we pair our trove of knowledge with a willingness to be inspired and improvise.

This middle phase is covered in nine chapters, beginning with Chapter 3, which describes how we identify and *track* the couple's negative cycles of interaction. We use tracking throughout the treatment to help the couple unblend from protectors and step back from content so they can notice how unmet needs, especially needs for safety, connection and love, fuel their fight. Once these needs have been identified, the partners can drop vertically into their personal payload of injury, safety lessons and trauma-based beliefs to do internal healing work. While the opportunity to do individual work can occur anywhere along the way in treatment, we cover it in Chapter 5.

But first, in Chapter 4, we describe how to teach the couple new communication skills that involve unblending so they can speak for parts and listen from the Self. In the practice of these skills we are most interested in the couple getting the feel of a regulated autonomic nervous system and developing enough trust to let the therapist become their *parts detector* (Schwartz, 1995) – the one who has permission to notice blending and call a time out in order to help the protector (or exile) unblend. In the role of parts detector we model de-shaming by getting curious about abhorred or disgraced parts. In general, to avoid shaming clients and gain their willingness, we alert them to our goals and get permission for the role we plan to play and the strategies we want to use. Because this invitation means that either partner can object, it's important to have other options handy and be willing to accommodate.

In Chapter 5 we cover the internal work of healing wounds. While this derives from IFS, working with a couple adds the element of relational unburdening. With individual work we begin by unblending protectors, but with a couple we also need to unblend the protectors of both partners so that one partner has the compassion to witness the other's injured, burdened part. When an individual feels closely connected to a young, vulnerable part and the partner resonates, extending love and care to that inner child, the moments of connection are healing. And when the partner is able to act as a compassionate witness (and sometimes a quiet cheerleader), the couple has a wonderful opportunity, born of the exquisite attunement generated by a Self-to-Self connection (Schwartz, 2008), to practice new communication skills.

In Chapter 6 we reach the heart of skills acquisition in this approach to therapy: the therapist's own practice of unblending, de-shaming and unburdening with the aid of the IFS therapy methods that we teach our clients.

Having set the table in Chapters 2 through 6 with unblending, self-regulating, learning new ways of communicating and unburdening past trauma, we turn back in Chapter 7 to those hard conversations about differences and needs that the couple came in with but did not have the skill to tolerate. Now that they understand each other's childhood dilemmas and are able to invite rather than threaten each other around meeting needs, the couple is ready to engage with an open heart. In Chapter 7 we walk them through negotiating needs, tolerating disappointment, and practicing new language and new behavior to get needs met, as well as mining the moments of connection that enable relational unburdening.

In Chapter 8 we unpack the issue of needs further, focusing on what happens when needs both correspond and conflict. All human beings need love and connection. Their hard-working protectors are often polarized inside (with other protectors) and outside (with their partner's protectors). Our goal is to help their protectors unblend and depolarize so the couple can become more skillful in this inevitable negotiation.

In Chapter 9 we offer a relational perspective on shame and review the key role of shaming and feeling shamed in all psychic burdens. We help couples understand the nature of shaming, how to break vicious cycles of shame and blame, and how to heal shamed parts.

In Chapter 10 we illustrate some of the creativity that we espouse throughout the book, deepening the couple's experience by challenging them to experiment with new behaviors in the therapy office.

In Chapter 11 we discuss what, from our perspective, makes difficult cases difficult. Being intimately attuned to our own internal systems and having the ability to unblend quickly and frequently is necessary for success in IFIO. Therefore, we hark back to Chapter 6, illustrating more of how the therapist's own personal work of unblending and developing the relationship between parts and the Self is key to responding to couples skillfully, no matter how they behave. Thus ends Phase 2.

Phase 3, covered in Chapter 12, prioritizes reconciliation and going forward. Bookending the broad, diverse middle phase of treatment, the ending, like the beginning, has a narrower focus: the practice of repair, resolution, forgiveness and the launch of a relationship that matches tolerance for – or perhaps celebration of – differences with love and mutuality.

The Three Phases of IFIO Couple Therapy

Phase 1: Beginning

- Meet the couple to assess their level of differentiation.
- Learn what they fear.
- Learn what they want, their hopes, desires and goals.
- Offer possibilities.

Phase 2: The Flow and Eddies of the Middle
What we do:

- Teach the couple new communication skills that will help them to unblend and regulate the autonomic nervous system.
- Get their permission to be in the role of *parts detector.*
- Track how they fight and how they are vulnerable, including:
  - how they negotiate needs;
  - how they shame each other;
  - how they receive shaming (how their protectors shame them).
- Walk the couple through the new communication behaviors that we want them to learn.
- Get them in their bodies and deepen their work with experiential exercises.

- Promote and reinforce relational unburdening.
- Do individual work, including:
  - unblending;
  - unburdening shame;
  - having the partner as a witness;
  - practicing new communication skills;
  - returning to relational needs;
  - practicing skills that are more likely to get needs met.

Phase 3: Ending

Here the therapist supports and guides as the couple, able to unblend, gradually takes over:

- Seeing the other as a resource rather than the *one who wounds* or the *redeemer*.
  - leading the process of repair;
  - addressing forgiveness.
- And, if they go forward, creating a relationship based on acknowledging differences as well as sharing a vision.

PHASE 1

BEGINNING

1

THE ORIGINS OF INTIMACY
FROM THE INSIDE OUT
THERAPY

Intimate relationships form the core of our social connections, helping us to grow, love deeply and tolerate loss (Bowlby, 1969; Coan, 2006; Johnson, 2004, 2013). When couples enter therapy in a state of disconnection, anger and grief at the loss of intimacy, they often hold two goals that feel like opposites: to feel safe and to reestablish intimacy. The IFIO approach offers a map for achieving those goals. In the following chapters we focus on how to create intimacy and explore what gets in the way, especially shaming and feeling shamed, as we illustrate how to work with the natural subdivisions – or *parts* – of the human mind in a dyad.

Since IFIO borrows concepts and a model of mind developed by Richard Schwartz and articulated in IFS, a review of those concepts is in order: Let's begin with *parts*. All models of mind that work with intrapsychic conflict deal in some form of mental multiplicity (see Freud (1961) on the id, ego and superego; Jung (1969) on archetypes and complexes; Assagioli (1975) on sub-personalities; Watkins and Watkins (1997) on ego state therapy; and various *inner child* approaches, among others). According to Schwartz, our parts think, feel, have beliefs, carry out everyday actions and are relationally sophisticated (1995). Each part has its own set of experiences. If left to manage their experience without guidance from a reliable parental figure, parts can become flooded with emotion, cognitively confused and burdened with intolerable beliefs. At this point some parts don a protective role and launch survival strategies that fit both the moment and the person's developmental age. These strategies, while useful in the moment, often prove far from optimal for quality of life and long-term growth.

No matter how dysfunctional their behavior looks once the crisis is over, these protective parts will endorse (for we can speak to them) altruistic motivation. They act in the service of survival, to the best of their ability, and the goal of treatment is to free, not to control or dismiss them. Luckily we can help our vulnerable, conflict-prone parts because we also have a *Self*. The Self in every one of us is capable of healing injured parts and leading our internal system with courage, wisdom and compassion (Schwartz, 1995). The concept of the Self aligns with *Buddha mind*, the *soul, inner light*, the *Tao* and *being in flow* as described in various spiritual and philosophical traditions. Although the Self is an energetic state available to everyone that cannot be wounded or damaged, it can be difficult to access, especially under troubled circumstances in childhood. The IFIO approach helps couples access the Self of each partner, extending this powerful resource, along with the concept of parts, into the relational setting as a vehicle for the growth and healing of both the individual and the couple.

Parts

So what are parts? Beyond subjective experience, we don't know. But when belief systems (including various religions, psychotherapeutic and self-help models) view parts as undesirable negative impulses they encourage people to ignore, shame or expel them from consciousness. Schwartz reports that his clients taught him to do the opposite: to welcome and listen to all parts. Our parts help us to survive; they enrich our lives with their intellect, gifts and talents; and they respond in kind when they are heard and valued.

Although we don't know what parts are, we can find them by paying attention internally to our thoughts, feelings, sensations and action urges. In doing so, we can notice that they shape our self-identity and motivate our behavior. And if we talk to them, they talk (or in some way communicate) back. Parts can describe how they absorbed interpersonal relationships as lessons and how they exist in relation to each other. From them, we hear that one part accepting relational injury as identity (*I am unlovable, I am bad*) motivates other parts to step into a protective role. Schwartz calls the former class of part *exiles* and the latter *protectors*. Further, he divides the tactics of protective parts into proactive (enacted by *managers*) and reactive (enacted by *firefighters*) (for more on the IFS vocabulary, see the Glossary).

IFS gives us a framework and language to know each part, regardless of its role in the internal family, and to understand the relationships between parts. Working with couples, as with individuals, we validate the choices parts have made given their circumstances, hear the ways in which their efforts were well intentioned, and assure them that we will not kill them off in the process of therapy. According to the tenets of the IFS model, which has been well confirmed in our experience, all parts have an inherent gift to offer the system once they have unburdened. This therapy welcomes all aspects of us, especially those parts who have been banished, and reunites them in the whole.

The Relational Options of Parts: Blending and Unblending

Because the relationship between parts and the Self fosters clarity and heals traumatic or just difficult experiences, developing that relationship is the principle goal of IFS therapy. Anything that interferes with it is seminal to the treatment, and the principal interference, true for couples as well as individuals, is *blending.*

Blending refers to a part taking over consciousness. Say you are driving home from work on a beautiful spring day, your window is down, the radio is on; you're singing along and looking forward to spending the evening at home. Suddenly a car pulls around from behind and cuts in too close. You slam on the brakes and swear, you're fuming and you notice an urge to chase the guy as he speeds away to give him a piece of your mind. From the point of view of IFS, an angry part has just taken over, or *blended*. Where did those carefree feelings go? Are they gone for good? Schwartz would say those feelings came from a part who has, for the moment, been supplanted in your consciousness. When the angry part calms down, the carefree one can edge back in and spread more joy.

This describes the natural activity of parts. They blend and unblend. They exert influence over consciousness and fade back in a practice similar to de-centering as described in mindfulness literature (Kabat-Zinn, 1990). When all goes well, parts share time and space with ease, receive support from the leadership of the Self and lend their support for the optimal functioning of the whole system. But when concerns for safety are uppermost and there has been little experience of Self-leadership internally or in role models, protective parts use what they have learned – often the very tactics to which they were unhappily subjected – to navigate and reestablish safety. The first phase of IFS therapy is devoted to befriending our protectors and showing them that they can unblend safely. If a part will not unblend and allow the client's Self to lead, then the Self of the therapist, which always models being Self-led in the therapy, can stand in for the time being.

The IFS Protocol with the Added Dimensions of IFIO

IFIO is an experiential model of couple therapy that was born over the last ten years as I applied the concepts of IFS to intimate relationships as a vehicle for the growth and healing of both the couple and individual. My model of couple therapy is designed to uncover the strengths and resources in each partner as well as in the couple in order to heal wounds that are current, that hail from prior relationships, or that occurred in childhood. And my goal is to nurture a healthy, intimate connection between partners as defined by them.

Guiding two people and their parts to interact in an open hearted, satisfying way when exiles are chronically triggered and protectors are hypervigilant and highly reactive is no small feat. As we illustrate throughout the book, couple therapy sessions encompass more parts and more people all at once than do therapy sessions for individuals. While individual IFS sessions differ, they generally involve *going inside* with one's attention to scan the body, listen for a voice, and/or see mental images. This internal focus tends to bring on a quasi-meditative state in which sensations, feelings or thoughts reveal a part or parts in need of attention. Since our job is to cultivate the cooperation of these parts and help them transform their modus operandi, we find various ways of asking them to unblend and be in relationship with the Self throughout the process. IFIO couple therapy makes use of IFS techniques and adds more to meet the needs of the larger relational system.

Healing the Intrapersonal and Interpersonal in IFIO

Because external relationships mirror internal relationships between parts and the Self, we integrate the interpersonal with the intrapersonal. While individuals from the couple do the interpersonal work of examining, healing, and reconnecting with their partner, they also do internal work, healing injuries and transforming toxic internal relationships. These two levels of process are mutually reinforcing and supportive. Intimacy is created from the inside out and vice versa, with an aim of generating loving and authentic yet adaptable, evolving relationships, both inter and intrapersonal.

As the introduction to this book explains, IFIO is organized around three phases of treatment. In the first phase, I meet the couple to assess their level of differentiation (their ability to accept being different from each other), inquire about their hopes and goals, and offer them my view of the possibilities. In the broad middle phase, I focus on helping the couple to differentiate, inside (from their parts) and outside (from each other), which in my view is key to their loving and being loved and to me helping them create the relationship they long for. This involves several actions that fall into one of the following categories: assessing patterns of behavior, teaching new skills (including new ways of communicating and making requests), and doing the individual work of unburdening.

To assess patterns of behavior, I start by tracking and understanding the vulnerability that motivates their fights in order to help them differentiate. Internally this means distinguishing the Self from parts, or unblending, which helps them regulate their autonomic nervous systems. I do this by asking them each to speak for rather than from their parts, which compels a significant measure of unblending. I also support them in understanding their emotional needs and being more skillful about getting those needs met. When we get to individual work, I help them to heal childhood wounds by unburdening shame. Throughout, regardless of which of these categories of action I find we are in, I work experientially to get them into their bodies, and I promote *relational unburdening*, healing that occurs between the couple that restores inner as well as outer relationships.

We reach the third phase of treatment when they are capable of seeing each other as a resource rather than as *the one who wounds* or *the redeemer* and engaging in repair. This renewed feeling of connection frees the couple to create the next chapter in their relationship, one that sees them consenting to (or embracing) difference and connecting in love.

Identifying Negative Cycles: Understanding the Fight

In IFIO we track how the emotional responses of young, frightened parts (called *exiles* in IFS) drive the responses of protective parts in the system. In other words, the therapist invites individuals to understand how what they do, or say, to their partner in an argument is driven by vulnerability and need.

Xander and Naomi

Naomi had a bad day at work and the kids began demanding attention as soon as she walked through the door. Though exhausted and overwhelmed, she was doing what had to be done: thinking about what to cook for dinner, feeding the dog and peeling carrots for the kids so they would stop eating cheese and crackers. And neither the kids nor her husband, Xander, seemed to notice or appreciate how hard she was working. A part inside felt alone, unappreciated and increasingly upset. Although this part wanted to be comforted by Xander, Naomi was blended with her busy manager mom part. Then she noticed that Xander had forgotten to take out the garbage … again. More evidence for the unappreciated part, who needed comfort and connection, that no one cared. So a protector got angry. And because Naomi's system was flooding with anger, she remained unaware of the needs of the part who felt uncared for and unappreciated. Instead she was thinking that Xander knew how much she hated to come home to full, smelly garbage bags in the kitchen.

Naomi wanted to feel valued and loved and her system understandably believed that Xander was the man for the job. But instead of telling Xander that she needed his attention and support she blew up. Her angry part was hoping that he would notice her need and come to the rescue, but she was not conscious of its agenda.

Unfortunately and understandably, Xander felt surprised and hurt by Naomi's anger. He had had a long day, too; he had just finished unloading the groceries he bought on the way home from work. A part of Xander was feeling, guess what? Overwhelmed and unappreciated. And now they were both in pain. He snapped back at Naomi, accusing her of attacking and nagging. Their disconnection sapped the pleasure of being home at the end of the day, of cooking together, of anticipating a good meal with their children, et cetera. Neither got what they wanted – and needed – from the other.

Why did this happen? Why do we get the opposite of what we hope for? We tend to operate under the illusion that our decisions are conscious, adult and based on present-day circumstances while, in fact, we respond according to past experience. The present and past are intertwined in the brain. When we feel threatened, a response is evoked in the amygdala, the primitive part of the brain that manages survival and safety. The amygdala stores *implicit memory*, the kind that exists without conscious awareness. For example, we know how to ride a bike or drive a car without conscious input. Implicit memories, which are also used for self-protection, are mostly formed in childhood, during times of high stress, or when survival is at stake. When implicit memories are evoked in the present, the brain responds as though it is the past (Cozolino, 2002).

Therefore, when a partner says or does something reminiscent of painful past experience the protective response is often powerful and lightning fast. When Naomi saw the overflowing garbage, a part who had felt unloved (and unlovable) felt that way again. In response, her protector attacked. This happened before she had a moment to remember that Xander did love her whether or not he took the garbage out. The speed at which we process emotional danger precludes evaluation, maturity and wisdom (Cozolino, 2002, 2008; Siegel, 2007). The crucial perspective we derive from the sense of time is overridden by threat. In the language of this model of therapy, a protective part tries to shield a highly activated internal system. In the language of neuroscience, activation of the amygdala operationalizes as either hypo- or hyper-arousal. Our clients are not making conscious choices and this is not a matter of fault. They are simply being human.

The starting gate of couple therapy, then, is typified by negative patterned arguments. These interactions are predictable regardless of content or who initiated the interaction. In IFIO, as in family systems therapy, we track cyclical behavior (Minuchin & Fishman, 1981). However, there is a difference between IFIO and the classic family therapy approach. Rather than just focusing on interpersonal interactions, we track internal interactions as well, focusing on how the behavior of protective parts is motivated by the emotional reactivity of frightened young parts (exiles). In other words, the therapist invites individuals to understand how what they do, or say, to their partner in an argument is driven by vulnerability and need. Tracking feelings and reactions inside and out is key, as we illustrate throughout the book.

Our Protective Parts in Relationship

Take a moment now to think about what happens to you when you feel hurt or scared in an intimate relationship. What do your protective parts tend to do: Run? Fight back? Stop listening? Intellectualize? Submit? Whatever tactic your protectors take, they have an uncanny knack for evoking exactly what you are hoping to avoid, just as Naomi did. Our protectors come on line developmentally as needed, but they stay with us and repeat the same old tactics in response to stress or threat even as our lives change. We may look and sound like adults but when our child parts respond to threats based on implicit memories, they take us along for the ride.

In IFIO we break this cycle by teaching individuals to do what Schwartz (2008) dubbed a *radical U-turn*, a strategy that develops the crucial relationship of the Self to parts. In the U-turn, the couple focuses primarily on their own reactions instead of their partner's behaviors. Let us warn you in advance that when protective parts hear the U-turn as a demand to suppress strong feelings and allow unacceptable behavior in the partner, you will get strong feedback. We illustrate various ways of executing the U-turn while helping protectors see it for what it is: an invitation to go inside and listen with curiosity and compassion.

The work in the case examples that follow includes one partner unblending to access the Self, which helps her regulate her autonomic nervous system, communicate more effectively and, finally, unburden shame. This kind of internal healing impacts the relationship directly (Schwartz, 1995).

Returning to the Conversation

After the U-turn we *re-turn*, bringing the focus back to the couple to help them remain unblended so they can more easily talk to each other about their hopes and fears, their past hurts, how their needs get met, and what they expect of themselves and each other. First the couple learns to recognize the vulnerable parts who lie beneath their conflict and then they learn to take care of their vulnerable parts, which allows them to be present with each other in a completely different way. This, too, we illustrate in the chapters to come.

A New Relationship

Reinstituting a loving relationship can heal the wounds that have been caused in relationship, which changes behavior, which changes the brain. Couple therapy, therefore, can offer a variation on unburdening that I call relational unburdening. When one partner bears witness internally to his young exiles, the other bears witness externally. Layered both in time and connectedness, this unburdening allows exiles to experience a contradictory, corrective experience (Ecker, 2012) inside and out.

Our goal is to guide couples toward mutual satisfaction, whatever that means for them. Rather than helping them to problem solve or find solutions to inevitable struggles, we want to foster connection with secure bonding, which reinforces open, caring interactions and appreciation for differences as well as similarities. When partners feel safe enough to understand and care about their parts and their partner at the same time, their interactions tend to shift dramatically. They can finally have those difficult conversations, the ones about safety, anger, sex, taking out the garbage, apology and forgiveness.

2

GETTING TO KNOW THE COUPLE AND INTRODUCING THE MODEL

In this chapter we illustrate a typical first session (or first few sessions) in which I get a feel for the couple, assess their level of differentiation, address their concerns about therapy as well as their hopes and goals, introduce them to the model and offer them a view of the possibilities. I also elicit the information that I want from them, including details about their early relationship, family of origin, way of fighting and apologizing (or not) and the baggage they carry now, ranging from life's normal stressors to bad luck or bad behavior.

The Role of the IFIO Therapist

In IFIO the therapist is active in the essential project of helping the couple to attain optimal arousal, which at times means doing whatever we can to prevent harm. With this goal, we listen for the emergence of parts (ours and theirs), notice the extent of blending, and especially tune in with protectors who attack or freeze. That is, we function as a parts detector (Schwartz, 2008) for the mini-system that includes the couple and therapist. To fulfill this role, we ask permission to prevent attacks by interrupting as often and as quickly as we deem necessary. In addition, we watch for parts who do the opposite of attacking and shut a person down by dissociating, going numb or checking out. This rarely happens during initial sessions but it is common later in therapy, and we illustrate it in the chapters that follow.

First Session with Susan and Marco

"What brings you here?" I asked.

"The last couple of years have been miserable," Susan began. "I don't even know what's happening, but we are having blow-ups more and more often ... and they last for days."

Marco nodded. "It's been tough. We do love each other, right Sue?" He glanced at her. "But we're hurting each other and we don't know how to put on the brakes."

Research indicates that the average couple is unhappy for six years before coming to therapy (Notarius & Buongiorno, 1992), by which time they feel discouraged, broken and sad. When we teach couples about parts and the Self it usually becomes easier for them to stay present with what is happening in the relationship. Over time, our goal is for them to learn to communicate skillfully, become less reactive, let go of burdens, make repairs and choose new behaviors with each other. The first meeting focuses on laying the groundwork for all this and creating as much safety as possible. Like all animals, we humans need safety. Because we scan for danger constantly (especially with a partner) and only the feeling of safety inhibits defensive reactions (Porges, 2007), we must prioritize creating safety for our clients.

At the outset of treatment I am mindful that this couple's story has developed over a period of time, often years, and each is likely to feel that her or his perspective has never been validated. Listening to them informs me about why they have come for help and how they behave in relationship. As I make sense of their experience I help them trust me and feel that change is possible. Throughout this therapy, the IFIO therapist is interested and non-judgmental, an essential stance if important issues and intense emotions are to be explored. At this early stage, our ability to mirror, reflect, normalize and validate is key. We listen. Over and over, we work on understanding what the couple is saying. We ask, *Am I getting this right?* In preparation for the next stage of therapy we also note patterns in how they relate.

In the following vignettes from an initial session with Susan and Marco, I establish what this couple wants and why they are seeking help. I also offer them possibilities for growth and change using IFIO. Some of the most common questions that I ask a couple in the beginning of therapy are bolded.

THERAPIST TIP

- Careful listening, tracking and reflecting back the stories that parts tell will anchor the couple's narrative in your mind.
- Gently asking your own therapist parts, who want to remain in the role of *expert*, to step aside will also help you to begin with the couple's presenting needs.
- The more slowly and deliberately you go, the more you will be able to track your own responses to what you hear.
- Staying attuned internally is key to staying present with the couple.
- Keep noticing which of your parts tend to get activated as you listen to your clients' stories.

Susan and Marco

"I used to think we had a good relationship but now I feel like Marco doesn't let me be myself," Susan began. "He criticizes me and pulls away."

"Oh come on Susan, *I don't let you?* That sounds like I'm your parent. You're being ridiculous," Marco replied.

Note that their language is blaming and judgmental and points to a storehouse of resentment and hopelessness, which is common at the beginning of treatment.

"What I hear," I interrupted, "is that things used to feel easier and recently there have been some dynamics, I think you mentioned *blow-ups*, which feel bad. And I hear, Susan, that you're feeling criticized. Is that right?"

"Yes," they said in unison.

"Can you tell me what was happening a couple of years ago when things began to feel difficult?" I asked.

The stressors they reported included their eldest child leaving home for college, an aging parent beginning to exhibit symptoms of Alzheimer's and Marco taking on more responsibility at work, which required him to spend more time away from home.

"It sounds like you've been facing a lot," I said. "Have you considered whether some of this is playing a part in what's happening between you?"

"I'm sure it is," Marco said.

"Given these stressors," I said, **"what happens when you have conflict?"**

"We fight all the time," Susan responded.

"What does that look like?" I asked.

"I feel like Marco is just looking for me to do something wrong."

"When you feel criticized, what do you do?" I asked.

"I shut down and stop talking," Susan said.

"And what happens to you, Marco?"

"I think she's too sensitive," he replied.

"And what do you say to yourself or do when you think she's being too sensitive?"

"I get annoyed I guess," he said.

"Sounds like a hard place to be. Given everything you've told me so far it makes sense that you need help. **What do you both hope will happen here?"**

They said they hoped for better communication, less conflict, and more connection.

Summing up, I said, "There is more exploring to do, of course, but what I understand at this point is that you would like help learning to communicate differently and you want to feel close again. **Am I getting this right?"**

Initial Questions from the Therapist

- *What brings you here?*
- *Can you tell me what was happening when things began to feel difficult?*
- *What's happening inside when you begin to feel emotionally overwhelmed?*
- *And then what do you say to yourself or do?*
- *Am I getting this right?*
- *Have you ever been in therapy together before?*
- *Would you like to explore your sexual relationship?*
- *Any history of alcohol or drug abuse?*
- *Any current life stressors?*
- *What is it like for you to be here today?*
- *What was and wasn't helpful in your last therapy?*
- *What are your goals for therapy, what do you both hope will happen here?*
- *How do you apologize and forgive each other?*
- *Do you have questions for me about how I work?*

Concerns About Therapy

As the couple's story unfolds, the therapist invites their questions and concerns, and listens in case one or both have parts who do not want to be there. Sometimes they will have had negative experiences with therapy in the past, sometimes their protectors will be anxious about what therapy will reveal. Sometimes, more strongly, one partner feels coerced or trapped.

If one or both express reluctance, the therapist will want to negotiate with that part. For example, you can suggest three or four sessions to precede making a commitment and let them know that, in any case, each person can decide to stop at any time. Questions like *What was and wasn't helpful in your last therapy?* And *What is it like for you to be here today?* draw out parts who might otherwise remain silent.

Couples may also have questions about the therapist and this model of treatment: *What training is required? What is the philosophy? What is your experience of success and failure using the approach?* Keeping the door open to all parts of the client helps create safety and connection. The work begins as soon as we are curious about their reservations to engage in therapy.

"Do you have questions for me about how I work?" I asked.

"I wouldn't know where to begin," Marco said.

"Have you ever been in therapy together before?"

"I saw a counselor years ago. Marco has never seen a therapist and we've never been in couple counseling," Susan replied.

"What's it like for you to be here today, Marco," I asked, turning to him.

"It feels okay I guess," he responded. "I'm not exactly comfortable if that's what you're asking. I had to be convinced this was a good idea."

"Do you have specific concerns about being here?"

"I know we need help, so I'm here for that. But I don't want to be ganged up on. You know, two women, one man – that sort of thing," he said.

"Thank you for speaking for that concern," I said. "I certainly wouldn't want you to feel ganged up on. So if you feel that way it would help me if you would say so."

"Okay," he said. "I will."

"Oh he will!" Susan said, smiling.

"How about you, Susan?" I asked. "Any concerns?"

"I feel more relieved than concerned to be here," she said.

THERAPIST TIP

- To create safety, we must invite our clients' concerns and welcome their parts who are not spoken for easily.
- Many people won't offer to speak of ambivalence, fear or skepticism; and they may be reluctant to admit having been wounded by a previous therapist.

- Inquiring about concerns can be liberating for the therapist as well. If the couple chooses not to return, having heard from parts who do not want to be there helps us to understand and accept that decision.

Goals and Wishes

The couple's goals and intentions, which inevitably change over time, guide our navigation and keep the therapy process on course. For example, a goal of wanting to change how they communicate permits us to point out dysfunctional patterns of communication. Conversely, being able to notice progress in relation to goals is invaluable in those difficult moments when partners feel they are going in circles with the same old material. For instance, *I can't keep going if he doesn't change*, or, *She's the problem – can you fix her?*

We should always make a point of listening to expectations, hopes and wishes, and following up by reassuring the couple that these concerns will be explored during therapy.

Susan and Marco

Couples early in therapy are often caught in a polarity between hopeless and hopeful parts. When the relationship feels stable or a therapy session goes well, hope dominates. With good timing, hope can be the midwife to change. But premature hope tends to deliver disappointment because of conflict or the feeling of incompleteness in therapy sessions. To defuse this polarity, I talk to clients about *possibility*.

"It sounds like both of you can get caught in feeling hopeful and then hopeless?" I said.

"The back and forth is just exhausting," Susan replied.

"I understand," I said. "In fact, it makes so much sense that I want to introduce a new idea. Instead of working hard to hold on to feelings of hope only to be disappointed, consider, for now, holding onto the *possibility of change* instead. Hope orients you to the future, while hopelessness keeps you focused on the past. In my experience, staying with what is possible right here and now, one step at a time, just focusing on your intention to change your relationship gives you some distance from the highs and lows of hopeful and hopeless parts. These are the feelings of parts who need your help and I can show you how to help them."

"I think I get caught in this cycle more than Marco," Susan said.

"No I can too," he said. "It's hard not to. It happens so quickly."

Early Relationship

If there is time in the first session or two, ask about the beginning of the couple's relationship. Going over how they met, what attracted them, what it was like to date, and how they fell in love can help them to soften and remember why they are together. It also evokes an important question: *What happened to us?* Here is how I might initiate this conversation.

Susan and Marco

"Tell me how you met and what first attracted you to each other."

They smiled at each other.

"You want to go first?" Susan asked.

"I remember the first time I saw Susan. I was awed. She was organizing a run and walk-a-thon for a summer camp program and I was running in the race. She was competent and gorgeous! Although I tried to get her attention, she ignored me," Marco recalled.

"I was up to my eyeballs in logistics! Also sweaty, dirty and exhausted. Not sexy."

"Oh yes, very sexy," said Marco.

"What happened?" I asked.

"He got my number from a friend. I didn't remember him but my friend had already called to order me to go out with him. So I did!"

"And?" I asked.

"He was great. Warm, funny, charming."

"What's it like to remember?" I asked.

"Sweet," said Susan.

"Sad," Marco said.

Introducing the Couple to the Concepts of IFIO

Typically while listening to their history and exploring their intentions, vision and goals, we begin to introduce the basic concepts of the IFIO approach and describe the ways in which our brains function relationally. Although some couples are more wary, others resonate immediately with the idea that the human mind is subdivided. They feel calmed by hearing that we all need connection but that needing produces vulnerability, which often summons frustration.

Our goal at this point is for the couple to begin to differentiate from their parts so they can tackle their problems with more objectivity and compassion. Since a little bit of explaining goes a long way, beginning to use parts language may be the most important teaching tool at the outset. Statements like, *I hear that a part of you feels X while another part feels Y* invites the couple to notice that they have parts, which is the first step in the long-ish process of learning to unblend (see Appendix 1 for an in-depth description of unblending), a topic that we mentioned at the beginning of the book and we continue to cover throughout.

When talk of parts having feelings makes a client balk, don't be discouraged. It's fine to search for acceptable language. For example, you can talk about *aspects of yourself, inner voices* or *thoughts, sensations and feelings*. Any language that helps the client explore her or his internal experience and absorb new concepts is fine.

Susan and Marco

"You both have a lot of parts – we all do. And just like the two of you, your parts don't always agree. Let me show you what I mean. You can both be defensive, right?" They nodded. "So take yourself back to the most recent time when you felt defensive, maybe today, and let me know when you're there.... Now what's happening in your body?"

After a moment, Susan said, "My stomach feels tight."

"Marco?" I asked.

"I don't know," he said.

"That's fine," I said. "What do you hear yourself saying to yourself...?"

"She's wrong," said Marco.

"Great. And you, Susan?"

"What a jerk."

"Now focus on those words and the feeling that goes with them. You can close your eyes if that makes it easier. What does this part of you want?"

"My anger wants Marco to respond," Susan said.

"Why?" I asked.

"Because I want to know he's listening," she replied.

"Your angry part wants Marco to listen to you?" I asked.

"Yes."

"How's that going?"

"Not very well."

"If I could help you find a way to relate so that you would be more likely to feel heard," I said, knowing the question was rhetorical, "would you be interested?"

The Concept of the Self

The concept of the Self and Self-energy can be harder for the uninitiated to grasp than the concept of parts because Self-energy is often in short supply when parts are in conflict. My views about the Self can also run awry of another person's religious or spiritual beliefs. Consequently, I introduce the concept of having a Self slowly, beginning either with their language or with vernacular synonyms for kindness and compassion, like *open heartedness* and *softening*. Here's what I might say in the first session if I have time.

"I'd like to talk to you about what I believe, which may also give you more information about how I work. I believe that all human beings have the desire to grow. I also believe we are essentially undamaged and have strong internal resources. This is not to say that you're not in pain. I know you're suffering. But it is to say that you have the capacity to bring resources of the heart to your own and to each other's hurts, anger, confusion and despair. At times I will ask you, in a variety of ways, to speak or listen from your heart."

How Do They Fight? Do They Apologize?

I also like to ask couples early on how they handle conflict in their relationship and if they are aware of what they do that frustrates or hurts the other person. This gives me information about how conscious their behaviors are and how attuned they are to the partner. In addition, asking about apology gives me information about injury that remains unhealed as well as the couple's capacity to repair and forgive.

Susan and Marco

"I'm curious how you fight," I said to Marco and Susan.

"We flare up," Susan responded. "Neither one of us really likes to back down but Marco will usually leave the conversation first."

I looked at Marco, who said, "She's right."

"Are you each aware of the behavior that hurts your partner most?" I asked.

"I think the worst for Susan is when I turn away," Marco said.

Susan nodded. "And I think my judging silence hurts Marco the most."

Marco nodded.

"And how do you apologize?" I asked them both.

"We don't," Susan replied. "I think that's part of the problem. We never finish a fight. I think there's been a build up of feelings over time."

Family of Origin

Family of origin is another important subject. Some couples have never pondered what they learned about relationships while growing up. Did their parents fight? If so, how? Did they resolve disagreements? What else did each partner see and learn as a child? The answers to these questions invite them to be curious about influences while helping us understand the origins of their dynamic.

Susan and Marco

"What did you learn about conflict from your early caregivers?" I asked.

Susan and Marco looked at each other knowingly.

"I learned to duck and run," said Marco. "Don't wait around to find out what's happening – get out quick!"

"And my parents just didn't fight in front of us," Susan said.

"Any models for apologizing?" I asked.

"Well," Susan laughed, "since we saw no fighting, we saw no apologizing."

"And I can't remember," Marco said.

"Does it make sense to you that all couples need methods for working through conflict and apologizing?" I asked.

Normal Stressors, Bad Luck, and Bad Behavior

Information about external circumstances, including children and extended family, is important. Many things will have affected the couple involving both normal phases of life and events over which they had no control. Are kids leaving home? Are parents moving in, or dying? Has someone lost a job? Maybe there are differences in libido, perhaps one of them is having an extramarital affair, or one of the partners has a mood disorder, a trauma history or an addiction. Since many couples will not bring up sensitive issues unless the therapist does, it's important to let the couple know that all topics are open for discussion. We cover the more explosive topics like rage and secrets in later chapters.

Susan and Marco

"There are a couple of questions I'd like to ask," I began. **"Do you want to explore your sexual relationship?"**

Susan and Marco looked at each other.

"Susan's not particularly happy about our sex life," Marco answered. "I know a lot of people struggle. But it's embarrassing to talk about and I can't imagine doing that with a third person."

There was a silence. Then Susan said, "We used to be so comfortable. Now it seems to me like Marco's just not interested and we can't talk about it without fighting. So it would help me."

"As we get to know each other I predict your conversations will change and you will feel more comfortable with me. Then I will help you explore your sexual relationship and understand what you each need in order to reconnect," I said.

Marco looked out the window. Susan nodded.

"Any other stressors?" I asked. "Illness, depression, aging parents, kids? Have either of you had affairs?"

If one partner chooses to disclose an affair in the first session, it can be extremely painful and difficult both for the listening partner and the therapist. However, because we work in the here and now, we address any situation that comes up head-on with as much Self-leadership as possible. In my experience this rarely happens but if it does the therapist must quickly calm her or his own system in order to remain present and available to the feelings of the couple.

"I haven't. Have you, Marco?" Susan said, turning to him.

"Nope," he said. "And we are childless by choice. We both have very high-powered jobs that we love and we chose that path instead of kids."

"Any stress from those jobs?" I asked.

"Yes. We're both under a ton of pressure."

Ending the Session

I always leave time at the end of a session to reflect on the essence of what I've heard and to explain how I might help.

"Before we end today," I said, "I want you to know that I hear your desire for different communication and I also hear that you have parts who have little faith that you can make those changes. **My job is to teach you how to have different interactions, ones that leave room for negotiating different needs as well as reconnecting in ways that you miss.** To that end, my job is also to create an environment that is safe enough for your protective parts to disarm. With time and hard work, I am confident your interactions can change."

THERAPIST TIP

- Take a moment to imagine redirecting someone who is blended with hopeless, angry parts in an initial session.
- Notice your body.
  - What is your impulse?
  - How do you feel?
  - What do you hear yourself saying to yourself?
  - What do you do?
- Holding your seat during uncomfortable interactions requires self-awareness and the ability to unblend quickly so that you can extend compassion and care to your own parts.

Summary

These case vignettes illustrate some of the questions I ask to determine external constraints, pressures on one or both partners, and any history of a serious breach of trust. In general, I gather information as I move forward, as illustrated in later chapters. It takes many sessions to get to know a couple's whole history, how they struggle and which dynamics they most want to change. Sometimes secrets or sensitive material emerge later on. Early or late, staying Self-led is key to hanging in with the unexpected and responding as needed.

All of the topics mentioned here can be covered in one long first session or over the course of a few sessions, and some may never come up. Some clients want to report. Others start to work on their issues immediately. Follow the couple and stay with their process. In my experience most couples make an attempt to remain calm and collected during the first session. They may be angry or frustrated but they want help and are willing to hold strong emotions back long enough to describe their situation and their struggles. Mirroring, connecting, creating safety and offering the possibility of change all help with the essential project of calming their autonomic nervous systems. As quickly as possible, we want to develop an alternative to the pattern of operating either from the fight or flight response of the sympathetic nervous system or from the slam-on-the-brakes, freeze response of the parasympathetic nervous system.

Therapists naturally have their own style and way of starting with clients. Each therapeutic venture launches a unique mini-system of couple and therapist in which all participants will inevitably develop a style of interaction and mutual accommodation. We do not suggest changing how you work unless it directly conflicts with the philosophy of IFIO. Keep your toolbox! The priority is to stay connected to your own parts and attuned to your clients' internal systems.

PHASE 2

THE FLOW AND EDDIES OF THE MIDDLE

3

TRACKING CYCLES

In this chapter we illustrate *tracking*, which I employ early on and return to as needed throughout treatment. Tracking is a powerful tool that was developed by the early pioneers in family therapy as a way of exploring patterns of behavior (Minuchin & Fishman, 1981), and adapted by Schwartz to track internal sequences. When we track their interpersonal and intrapersonal interactions, we help the couple unblend and notice how their behavior has more to do with unmet needs, especially for safety, connection and love, than with whatever content they keep repeating in their fights. We also illustrate how I work with goals early in treatment. If they are focused on changing each other, I clarify that our process will never be about one person changing so the other can stay the same.

Why Track?

We do not solve problems in IFIO. Rather, we assist the couple in developing the skill to problem solve well. Therefore, we are interested in motivation, not content. We want to move the couple from focusing on the content of their fight to feeling curious about what motivates their fighting. In IFIO one of our first moves is to track behaviors that are driven by intense emotion because it slows the couple down, clarifies recurring patterns, and helps us to highlight the vulnerable, exiled parts whose feelings trigger their problematic behavior.

Negative Cycles

In uncomfortable situations everyone has a preferred way of showing up. Protective parts may withdraw, argue, submit, explain, get on the cell phone, rage or engage in any number of other behaviors designed to distract from and minimize emotional pain. We define a negative cycle as a predictable pattern of interaction that gets repeated regardless of content and outcome. Needless to say, negative cycles are destructive and exhausting. Tracking the cycle interrupts the behavior and reveals, often for the first time, the hopes of the protector and the needs of the exile. We return to tracking repeatedly during treatment to highlight the ways in which the underlying motive for the cycle is more important than the content of the couples' arguments. Our goal is for each member of the couple to do the U-turn and engage in self-exploration. That is, we aim to move their focus inward and off their partner, especially in the beginning.

THERAPIST TIP

Before reading this illustration of tracking, close your eyes (if that helps) and imagine yourself seated in front of a couple. Notice what you feel, invite your parts to trust you, and then imagine going through this interaction slowly, listening and reflecting back.

Sophie and Sam

"I need help," Sophie reported during a session early in treatment. "I can't make a simple request without Sam responding like an overgrown teenager."

"A request?" Sam shot back. "You make demands. You're always trying to control me."

"And your passive aggressive behavior isn't controlling?" Sophie snapped.

"Sweet!" Sam replied, shifting to face away from her.

To gain information about this couple's way of relating during conflict, I waited a few moments before interrupting. Couples come into my office in one of two ways: either they are reporting a typical cycle of interaction or they are in it. Having them in the cycle, though sometimes intimidating, is easier in the sense that their parts arc present and accessible. Sam and Sophie were in the middle of their cycle.

"Sounds like your dilemma is unfolding right here, right now," I said.

They looked at me.

"So you see what I mean," Sophie said. "He thinks it's my fault. And, frankly, I think it's his fault."

Many clients come in blended with a strong manager who hopes the therapist will recognize the ways in which the partner is the cause of all the trouble. In this fantasy, the therapist will work to change the partner and everything will be resolved. We know that relational problems are co-created and co-maintained but this knowledge precludes easy answers and can be hard to hear. Humor can help put the fantasy in perspective and level the playing field.

"Wouldn't it be great if someone could wave a wand and change Sam?" I said to Sophie. "But," I added, turning to Sam, **"I bet you'd like Sophie to get the wand treatment, too."**

"I would!" he said, glaring at Sophie.

"Of course you would. But," I looked to Sophie, "joking aside, I hear you're frustrated. You make requests of Sam and his response is hard for you."

"At best he says *No*, at worst he walks away as though I haven't even spoken!"

At this point a traditional couple therapist might turn to the partner for input, but I stayed with Sophie for a little longer because I wanted her to begin to learn to track her internal experience instead of thinking about what she wanted from Sam.

"When he says *No*, or walks away," I said, "what happens inside you? What do you hear yourself saying to yourself?"

"I hear myself saying, *What is the point?* I'm not dealing with an adult. I get furious!"

"Are you feeling furious right now?" I asked.

"I am mad," she said.

"Would you be willing to stay curious with me for a moment about this part who feels mad?" I asked.

"I guess so."

"Do you notice it somewhere in your body?" I asked, knowing that asking her to stay with emotion in her body would both slow her down and intensify the feeling.

"There's a tightening in my chest and arms. My body is clenching up," Sophie said.

"So you make a request of Sam that feels reasonable to you, he responds by saying *No* or walking away and you get frustrated, which you notice as a tightening in your chest and arms, am I getting it right?"

"Yes."

"And then what does your mad part do or say to Sam?"

I use this very important question often. While some people cannot describe feelings and are unaware of the body, they know what they do.

"I try to get him to listen."

"How do you do that?"

"By raising my voice."

I turned to Sam, "Do you know that part of Sophie?"

Tracking involves moving back and forth between partners in this way to highlight their cycle. If you plan to focus on one partner for a few minutes, first ask permission from the other partner, or just let the other know that you will be back shortly. Then, even as you focus on one, be sure to make eye contact with the other. Because this can be hard to remember, it's important to practice until it becomes second nature.

Sam nodded, "Very familiar."

"And what do you notice inside when she raises her voice?"

"I get angry too."

"And what do you hear yourself saying to yourself?"

"I'm outta here!"

"And then what do you do or say?"

"I pull away."

"So Sam, **when Sophie raises her voice, you get angry, too, and you get out of there**, is that right?"

"Yes."

"And Sophie, **when Sam pulls away, what happens inside you?**"

"I have the urge to get louder."

"And **when you get angrier and louder, what happens with Sam?**" I asked.

"He disappears."

"Sounds painful," I said, "because clearly you both end up feeling frustrated, angry and alone."

"And not understood at all," Sophie said.

"I don't feel respected," Sam said.

THERAPIST TIP

- Tracking involves moving back and forth between partners to highlight their cycle.
- Resist the urge to get involved in the content of their argument, which may (or may not) be important later on.
- But while tracking do reflect back to them what you're hearing to reassure them that you're listening carefully and that you understand them both.
- If you plan to focus on one partner for a few minutes, let the other know that you will be back shortly. This keeps the work primarily horizontal.
- Then, even as you focus on one partner, keep making eye contact with both.

"Is this the way you normally fight?" I asked.

"We do this over and over," Sophie said.

"Good. **This illustrates very well how a protective part in one of you brings out a protector in the other.** And on and on it goes." Since my next interest was to explore the hopes and fears of their protectors, I continued, "Shall we take a look at what fuels your protectors?"

They nodded.

To keep Sophie from feeling like the identified patient, I looked over to Sam. "Shall we start with you?"

He shrugged.

"How familiar are you with the part who wants to pull away?"

"Very," he said. "It's my default when I feel controlled."

"What is it afraid would happen if it were to let you stay in the interaction?"

He considered before saying, "I would lose control."

"Of what?"

"Me."

"Say more," I invited.

"Hmmm..." he said. "I was very controlled as a child though my parents had different ways of doing it. My father was angry and my mother was passive. And she controlled him silently."

"And what is this part afraid would happen if it didn't pull you out of the interaction with Sophie?"

"I'll get pushed around and squashed."

"And then what?"

"I'll feel small and used."

"Small and used is unpleasant," I said. **"Does this part prevent those feelings?"**

"Not always," he said.

"Did it work in your childhood?"

"I felt the feelings but going away protected me," he said.

I turned to Sophie, **"How familiar are you with your part who gets angry and loud?"**

"It always shows up for me," she said.

"And what is this part afraid would happen to you if it didn't show up?"

"I'd be ignored."

"Does that make sense to you?"

"Yes," she said. "I felt invisible a lot in my childhood. Nobody in my family listened to anyone who didn't barge in and get loud."

"So you do with each other what you learned to do to survive a long time ago."

Note that the couple has now identified their vulnerable parts who are being protected. Although it's tempting to stay with those vulnerable parts, doing so early in the therapy could derail the process. First, the therapist can get caught up prematurely with one partner, causing the other to feel abandoned. Second, protectors generally need to feel fully heard before they can tolerate the therapy focusing on exiles. So at this stage we just notice the existence of exiles and return to tracking protectors.

THERAPIST TIP

- Staying with vulnerable parts (exiles) during the initial tracking of protectors can derail the process.
- First, the therapist can get caught up prematurely with one partner, causing the other to feel abandoned.
- Second, protectors need to feel understood before they can tolerate the therapy focusing on exiles.
- So in the beginning we notice the existence of exiles and return to tracking protectors.

"Can you see that this cycle is about something vulnerable in each of you?" I asked.

"I can't say I knew that," said Sophie.

"It makes sense to me," Sam said.

Although Sam and Sophie were able to unblend enough from their protectors to recognize that vulnerable feelings were driving their conflicts, not all couples are able to do this so quickly. That's fine. We just stay with protectors until they reveal what motivates their behavior.

Now it was time to invite them to think about responding to each other differently, so I said, "What if we could help your protective parts feel less need to react strongly? **What if, regardless of the other person's response or reaction, you could maintain the sense of being connected inside and choose how to respond?**"

Sam's answer was not uncommon, "Sounds like what you're really saying is I should stand there and take whatever's coming. I'm not doing that."

Using a method Schwartz calls *direct access* (1995) in which I spoke directly to his protector without pausing to get Sam's Self talking with this part, I said, "I understand why you might think I'm saying that. Let me try again. **I'm suggesting a new kind of interaction in which both of you are less reactive, less powerless, less angry and less invisible.** When Sophie gets mad, what if your protector didn't feel it had to take you out? And, Sophie, when Sam isn't responsive, what if your protector didn't feel it had to go off like a rocket? **I want you to consider the idea that important issues can be approached more effectively so that you can actually have these difficult conversations instead of avoiding them.**"

"So how do we do this?" Sophie said.

THERAPIST TIP

- Pay attention to your own parts and learn how to help them unblend.
- Hold warmth and compassion for the couple's protectors and yours no matter how they present.
- Don't get stuck in content: track their interactions.

Although one partner often believes the other starts the fight and feels that she or he has no choice but to react, we know that we're dealing with a cycle and it's not important who started the fight. When overtaken by strong emotion, people feel compelled into action because every emotion comes hard-wired with an urge for action. We work on unblending from parts with strong emotions because, in the long run, having to act on an emotion is disempowering. In contrast, the capacity to regulate strong emotion, which develops when the person's Self and her parts are in good relationship, is empowering. Although I had not yet focused on the concept of having a Self with Sophie and Sam, I was asking questions that I hoped would encourage their parts to differentiate and make room for their Self-energy. For example, **"If you did have a choice to respond differently, what might you do?"** and **"Would you like that?"**

Now curious about how to have different interactions, Sam and Sophie were calmer. This meant they were more open minded, open hearted and physiologically prepared to connect. In a small exchange with some tenderness, they agreed that they did want to respond differently. When you notice a moment like this, slow down and idle. Since relationships always cycle, positive cycling is our goal. When we see it, we slow down to reinforce it. In the chapters that follow we illustrate the answer to Sophie's question: "So how do we do this?"

Summary

The purpose of tracking a couple's cycle is threefold. First, by staying horizontal and going back and forth between members of the couple to flesh out their dynamic, we help them see that their fight is repetitive, predictable and circular in nature. Second, we want them to understand that their fight is motivated by strong feelings. Tracking slows them down so we can help them look inside and understand the hopes and fears of their protectors. Third, we make an invitation to both partners to consider how their interactions would be different if they experienced less reactivity and more choice in responding. Throughout we encourage them to try something different.

A Road Map for Tracking Cycles (feel free to copy and use)

Steps to Take in Tracking:

- Reflect back what you hear them saying.
- Describe their cycle.
- Introduce parts language.
- Slow down to introduce the U-turn:
  - *When your partner says or does that...*
  - *What happens in your body?*
  - *What happens inside you?*
  - *What do you say to yourself about yourself or about your partner?*
  - *What do you do or say to your partner?*
- Attend to one partner and then the other until they recognize the cycle.
- Explore the hopes and fears of their protectors.
  - *What are you afraid would happen if you didn't do this?*
  - *What is your hope by continuing this behavior?*
- Name the exile, if possible.
- Extend the invitation:
  - *Would you be interested in being less reactive and having more choice in how you respond when your partner does that thing?*

Unblending Techniques

We can also help couples to externalize their parts. Visuals promote unblending.

Here are some options for incorporating visuals:

- Draw or map parts on a whiteboard or on paper. Illustrate the relationship between protectors and more vulnerable parts.
- Use figures in a sand tray.
- Use other objects (scarves, pillows, pebbles, etc.) that they can manipulate in space.

4

COURAGEOUS
COMMUNICATION

In Chapter 4 we explore how couples communicate and offer options to change their conversations. Often one or both partners become too dysregulated to speak or listen effectively. Since remembering childhood injury together generally evokes empathy, we illustrate how to help the couple unblend and become curious about the ways in which a partner's behavior in the present relates to the past. As the reader will see, this task can go easily or not. If not, the therapist must bring genuine kindness and curiosity as well as providing firm direction in the project of helping the couple regulate and be available to each other. Success supports them in finding common ground so they can express more love and care, which in turn reinforces skillful communicating.

The Importance of Communication

Robust data in attachment research show that human beings thrive on connection. *Contingent communication* (Seigel, 2007) is the heart of secure attachment, meaning one person *feels felt* by another. To unpack this concept, we could say: I experience you tuning in and sending me the message *I am with you*. We can tune in verbally, non-verbally or both. Empathic communication like this wires and rewires the brain (Seigel, 2007).

At the outset of treatment, after tracking a couple's negative cycle and demonstrating its futility, I always ask, **"If I could help you learn to communicate in a different way, would you be interested?"** Because most couples are desperate for help, they will agree to be interested in changing their style of communication. But their compliance at this point is uneducated and they don't yet know how much courage it takes to hold back parts who feel empowered, at least in the short run, by behaviors like attacking and withdrawing.

Even so, I know that behind this need for immediate relational impact, no matter what words a couple uses, no matter what demands they place on each other, each is really saying, *Do you hear me? Am I safe with you? Will you meet my needs?* Since their protectors already believe the answer to these questions is *No!* they are perpetually on the alert for abandonment or attack. As a result, they easily mistake a feeling (*I'm being attacked*) for fact. We honor the urgent concern and good intentions of protectors, even as we use various tactics to help them unblend so the couple can inhabit a broader perspective.

Learning to Do What's Difficult

The goal of treatment in IFIO is to part *difficult* from *wounding* and help couples do what's difficult skillfully. We believe that a couple will be able to tolerate difficult conversations and solve their own problems once they learn to conduct vulnerable interactions safely.

Courageous Communication

Intimate relationships require good communication, which ultimately means being able to stay in a conversation that involves differences long enough for both people to feel heard and understood. This does not mean coming to an agreement. Many couples new to therapy have little capacity to stay with an issue until each person feels fully heard. Instead they have parts who either negotiate their differences unskillfully, like problem solving parts who hope for quick solutions and an end to conflict, or parts who interrupt to shut the other person up, or parts who appear to comply in order to end the conversation. These parts make requests that are really shaming and blaming demands like, *If you would only . . .* or, *Why don't you just . . .*, which naturally backfire. In IFIO, we teach clients new ways to process content, which changes the outcome of their conversations.

Courageous communication involves responsible self-disclosure, which means taking the risk of revealing private information, vulnerabilities and uncomfortable responses without criticizing or shaming internally or with the partner. We want clients to feel confident about conducting hard conversations with no need for the protection of parts who wound and alienate. However, this tall order takes time.

Couple therapists will notice that the more reactive the couple, the less internally differentiated the individuals in the couple. Highly reactive couples need significantly more help with the internal process of unblending. In the service of teaching them to unblend, we move back and forth between internal and external relationships. The U-turn helps each partner develop internally differentiated relationships; the *re-turn* to their relationship teaches them to speak on behalf of parts instead of from them, after which they are better able to listen from the Self with openness, curiosity and compassion. Over time, this more skillful behavior helps them to respond calmly to conflict and rupture when it does occur.

THERAPIST TIP

- The U-turn develops internally differentiated relationships.
- The re-turn involves speaking on behalf of parts instead of from them.
- Listening from the Self is characterized by openness, curiosity and compassion.

The Imago Dialogic process developed in the 1980s by Harville Hendrix inspired, at least in part, my methods of courageous communication. Imago dialogue was designed to create safety and recognize the wounding from childhood beneath troubled interpersonal dynamics. While I borrow some of Hendrix's techniques, my approach is uniquely focused on differentiating parts from the Self and cultivating that internal relationship, which in turn supports healthy external differentiation and attachment between partners. Additionally, teaching clients to use classic relational techniques like mirroring and validating with their own parts as well as with their partners helps us to locate any parts who are in danger of feeling coerced, left out, ignored or shamed by the therapy process. These are the parts who cause trouble when the couple leaves your office, or later in treatment.

Listening Skills

- Hear your partner's experience before deciding what's true or reacting.
- Hear about your impact on your partner without disagreeing or engaging in self-attack.

Supporting the Listener

Since we all have more space to evaluate our behavior honestly when we are able to separate from and speak on behalf of our parts (Schwartz, 2008), we assist people in learning good listening skills. These include postponing consideration of what feels true until one has heard the other person's experience without reacting, and hearing about one's impact on others without disagreeing or engaging in self-attack. The case below illustrates how to help a couple move from poor communication and misunderstanding to speaking for parts and listening with curiosity.

Seamus and Lori

"I can't work with your mess and disorganization," Seamus said to Lori.

"You should learn to chill out," Lori replied. "You've got OCD."

"You see? She never listens to me. This always happens. When I ask for something I have a mental disorder. I'm sick of it," Seamus sighed deeply, looking at me.

A plea to be heard or a complaint about not being heard signals that the couple is not communicating skillfully, which is an opportunity to offer them new ideas about speaking and listening.

"Sounds to me like communication that needs to happen between you two isn't going well?" I asked rhetorically.

"I don't feel heard," Seamus said.

"I don't either," Lori snapped.

"When you try to communicate, do you both end up angry and defensive?"

They nodded.

"What if there was another option?" I said. "What if you, Seamus, didn't feel you had to get angry to be heard? And what if you, Lori, didn't feel you needed to defend yourself? Would you be interested? **In other words, what if something could happen here in this office that made it possible for you to talk about what you need without going after each other?**"

"Yes, of course," Lori said.

Seamus nodded but looked skeptical and tired.

THERAPIST TIP

- Some people struggle with unblending as they begin this new method of speaking and listening.
- Validate frequently and remain available to assist. If a partner cannot respond with kindness or understanding, be the model for empathy and attunement yourself.

Start with the Listener

Listening without formulating a response while someone else speaks is a skill. Partners in reactive couples are more likely to be engaged with their internal conversation than to be listening to an external one. Since feedback from a partner is a particular challenge, we take time to orient the couple to the role of listener, helping the one who steps into this role become available by unblending busy protectors.

"Who wants to speak first and who wants to listen?" I asked.

"Since Seamus is obviously so upset with me right now," Lori said, "I'll listen."

Once the couple decides, I explain the role of listener: **"The job of listener is potentially harder than the job of speaker because negative statements trigger protective parts. If that happens, I'm here to help. When someone else is unhappy with you, attacking or submitting are not the only options. I'm here to help you remember that you're hearing someone's experience of you, not the truth about you,"** I said.

Introducing the Job of Listener

- *The job of listener is potentially harder than the job of speaker because negative statements trigger protective parts. If that happens, I am here to help.*
- *When someone else is unhappy with you, attacking or submitting are not the only options. I am here to help you remember that you are hearing someone's experience of you, not the truth about you.*

"And Seamus," I said, **"while I'm talking to Lori about listening to you, I encourage you to check in with yourself and pay attention to your** *intention.* **What do you want her to understand?"**

Turning back to Lori, I said, **"It isn't always easy to listen and I appreciate your willingness. I invite you to scan your body –**

especially around your heart – and pay attention to any parts who might have feelings about you listening to Seamus."

In my experience this inquiry, if done gently and respectfully, invites parts who are compliant or feel controlled, angry or afraid to speak up, unblend and participate. This is especially important with shame protectors, who are always on guard. When we help them to unblend at the outset, we don't have to start and stop repeatedly to help the listener remain unblended.

Instruct Both Listener and Speaker to be Internally Mindful

- To the speaker:
  - *While I'm talking to Lori about listening to you, I encourage you to check in with yourself and pay attention to your intention. What do you want her to understand?*
- To the listener:
  - *Scan your body – especially around your heart – and pay attention to any parts who might be getting in the way of listening to Seamus.*

"I'll give it a go as long as he doesn't attack me," Lori said.

"Sounds like you have a part of you who is afraid of feeling attacked," I said.

"Yes I do," she replied. "Especially since that's how Seamus communicates!"

"It's my job," I said, **"to help you speak to each other responsibly and prevent attacks. If either of you has difficulty speaking or listening without attacking, blaming, or shutting down, I will call a time-out and we'll slow down so I can help you."**

"That helps," Lori said.

"Noticing your body will give you a sense of how available you are to your parts and to Seamus. Check to see if there are parts who feel stirred up around your heart or belly."

"I'm okay," she replied.

"One more thing," I said. **"Keep in mind that this is his experi- ence of you and not the truth about you. If you can receive what he has to say as information about Seamus and not the truth about you and your parts, you may hear things you didn't know."**

"Fair enough," she said. "I can listen."

"Great." Turning to Seamus, I asked, "What have you been noticing as I was speaking to Lori?"

"This feels a bit controlled," he observed.

Protectors may resist sampling this skill set because close, mindful attention to intention and to speech takes them out of the driver's seat. For a blended part, this can feel too disempowering.

"I understand," I said to Seamus. "I'm asking you to try some- thing that doesn't come naturally. **But if you are willing to prac- tice, especially here with me, your protectors can learn to rely on you and relax so that your conversations can change. I want you to practice mindful speaking and listening until it feels nat- ural and intuitive."**

"Okay," he said. "I'll give it a try."

"Were you able to think about what you want Lori to know?" I asked him.

"I was."

"Can you find the part who you are going to speak for in or around your body?" I asked.

"Yes," he said.

"And so that Lori can listen more easily, I am going to invite you to speak *for* instead of *from* this part."

THERAPIST TIP

- Remember:
  - The couple is one system consisting of two individu- als, who each have injured parts *and* a Self who is whole and unburdened.
  - You also have a Self who is whole and unburdened.

> • As you move from one partner to the other helping
>   each to unblend, notice your own body and ask
>   yourself:
>   • *How unblended am I now?*

"It's funny," he said, "as you were talking to Lori, I did have time to reflect on something."

"What was that?" I asked, interested that he had been able to unblend while listening to my conversation with Lori.

"There's something about the messiness in the house that agitates a part of me. I think this part is already overwhelmed from a day at work and then I can't find a peaceful place – not in myself or in the house or with Lori."

"And then what?"

"I blame her. I think you should know this about me after all these years," he said, turning toward her.

"And what is hard about telling her what you're feeling when you come home?" I asked. But before he answered, I turned to Lori, "I am going to ask you to stay curious with me and listen to what he says."

After a long pause he said, "It's embarrassing."

"Seamus, this part of you who feels embarrassed to tell Lori what's happening for you – what is it embarrassed about?"

He was quiet for a moment and then said softly, "I think it's about feeling overwhelmed and needing help."

This sudden drop to vulnerability surprised both Seamus and Lori – but not me. When protectors are treated with respect instead of as unwelcome intruders they will sometimes soften suddenly, allowing the truth of exiles who feel shamed and vulnerable to emerge (Schwartz, 1995).

"Can you speak for the embarrassed part now?" I asked Seamus.

He turned to Lori, "Boy, did I learn as a kid that asking for anything was futile. It may sound strange but I guess it never occurred to me that I could get what I need by asking you."

Acutely aware of the risks of this moment – any response to this kind of disclosure other than understanding, mirroring or acknowledgment will be shaming and can evoke protection (Seigel, 2003) – I looked to see Lori's response. She was gazing attentively at Seamus.

"What are you hearing?" I asked her.

"It sounds like you're really stressed, Seamus," she said. "And when I leave the place messy it makes things worse." He nodded. "I know it's hard for you to ask me for anything and I know you came from a family with a lot of macho men. But I feel closer to you when you let me know what you need."

Seamus's willingness to speak for vulnerable feelings meant Lori didn't feel attacked, which allowed her protectors to stop defending her disorganized part. Instead, feeling empathic and interested in his experience, she responded to his need.

"How do you feel, hearing that?" I asked him.

"Relieved," he said.

"And you?" I asked Lori.

"I love Seamus," she said simply.

"Is there anything else you'd like to say before we stop today?"

"Seamus," Lori said, "if you can ask me for help rather than criticizing me for being messy I'm pretty sure I can be a lot less reactive."

"I wish it weren't so hard," Seamus replied. "This is really hard for me."

"I agree it can be hard," I jumped in. "Especially if you have parts who believe that asking for help is futile. For today, let's say we have much more to explore – and we'll take time to do that."

It's Not Always this Easy

Because Lori and Seamus were interested, they were able to try something new with my help. This is not always the case. Some couples become overwhelmed, causing their protectors to revert to muscular tactics of blaming, accusing and manipulating.

Over time I have come to appreciate that a protector's job is to stay focused on the other person because the interaction is evoking feelings that are all too reminiscent of a painful past. Helping partners feel safe enough inside to listen to each other can therefore take many attempts. The foundation of this kind of work is long-term patience and persistence of the therapist (Schwartz, 1995). In the vignette below we illustrate how compassionate perseverance helps highly reactive parts begin to trust the therapeutic process.

Luke and Adrienne

"I notice each time we try to have this conversation that both of you get agitated and overwhelmed quickly, so I'd like to begin differently this evening," I said. "Let's start with taking a moment to breathe deeply.... Notice your body. Does it feel tense, agitated, tight? Or are you relaxed, available? What do you hear yourself saying? Are there parts who urgently want to be heard or who feel like getting out of here?"

By getting Luke and Adrienne to notice, and therefore begin to unblend from, the physical and mental states caused by blending parts, these questions invited them into a U-turn. "We'll hold off speaking until each of you is connecting, at least in some small way, to yourself," I said. "Notice your parts. Who needs to be heard? What needs to happen inside so your parts can trust you today?"

Luke was able to close his eyes for a short time, which was new. Adrienne closed her eyes, her breathing slowed and she looked comfortable. Although this opening helped them ground themselves (and helped my parts who were anticipating that they would attack each other and probably me as well) it was not a match for their intense dysregulation and shame, and, as we will see, they were not able to stay unblended.

"Who would like to start?" I asked.

"I will," Adrienne said.

After helping Luke prepare to listen and assuring him I was there to help, I said to Adrienne, "As you notice what you want to say, let me remind you about speaking for your parts instead of from them."

"I'll try," she nodded. Turning to Luke, she began "I have a lot of feelings about this, as you know."

"I know," he said.

"I get upset really quickly." She took a breath. "I have a lot of built up resentment." She took another breath.

"Is there more those parts want you to say on their behalf?" I asked, nudging her parts to stay unblended.

"What are you doing with your face, Luke?" she snapped. "I know you're not listening to me. You see," she said, turning to me, "he's never going to listen to me." Turning back to him and raising her voice, she went on, "You clearly don't care about me or about having this conversation!"

I glanced at Luke, who looked startled. Before he could respond, I turned back to Adrienne and said "What just happened?"

Note that I asked *What just happened?*, not *What are you doing?* and not *How are you feeling?* because, in my experience, *What just happened?* puts the breaks on an aggressive protector non-judgmentally and/or diverts its attention from the partner.

Turning to me, she said, "I've been quiet long enough. You're not going to stop me! I know when Luke is checking out. I can read him like a book."

In my response below, watch for the four distinct steps I use with aggressive parts: **validating** her protector's anger, **confronting** its behavior kindly and firmly, **warning** it about unwanted consequences and **offering an alternative**, including my help. Also note that I used direct access to speak to her angry part.

"**I understand that you want and need to be heard. Your anger makes complete sense to me.** *[Validation]* However," I paused for effect, looking her in the eye, "**communicating this way won't get you what you want.** *[Confrontation]* Adrienne's face relaxed slightly. I went on, "**If you shame Luke, he will have no choice but to stop listening to you and shut down.**" *[Warning about unwanted consequences]* I glanced over at Luke, who nodded.

Adrienne took a breath, her shoulders dropped and her jaw relaxed. I knew her part was giving way.

"I do believe," I went on, "that what you have to say and the meaning behind it are important. Will you let me help you speak to Luke in a way that he is more likely to be able to hear and take in?" [*Offering an alternative*]

> ### Four Steps for Intervening with an Aggressive Protector
>
> - Validate its anger.
> - Confront its behavior kindly and firmly.
> - Point out the inevitable, unwanted consequence(s).
> - Offer the alternative – including your help.

"Thank you for saying my anger makes sense. I do want your help," she said, "but I deserve to have my feelings."

"Yes indeed you do," I said, validating her angry part again.

"Speaking *for* my feelings is just a way to damp them down. There is no authenticity in that," her angry part complained.

Many people have protectors who believe that anger can only be *authentic* if expressed with aggression; they also believe that only aggression gets results. Over and over, I challenge these beliefs.

"I have a different view," I said. "I believe authenticity is best captured when you are strong and clear. Speaking for your parts is a good way to be assertive and it's a handy way to be strong and clear. Would you be willing to give it a try with my help?"

She nodded with some hesitance, as if over some internal objection.

"And Luke, what are you noticing as you listen?" I asked, turning to him.

"I was noticing that Adrienne has strong feelings," he replied calmly.

"Can we begin again?" I asked.

With some couples, the therapist needs incredible patience and determination to remain steady, as well as faith that as parts unblend Self-energy will show up to facilitate different conversations.

The Purpose of Introducing Courageous Communication

• Promotes unblending and neural regulation.
• Helps the couple move safely from content to process.
• Helps the protective system to trust that a different way of communicating can bring relief.
• Invites vulnerable parts to be seen and heard.

Helping Couples Communicate Well about Sensitive Issues

The tools described here can be employed to promote clear, respectful communication when couples who are driven by protectors have sensitive, tender issues to discuss. For example, the case below illustrates how I work with differences in desire, one of many issues related to sexuality that couples can face. Before moving into the case, however, here is an important caveat: Sexuality is a vast, complex topic. Depending on the issue involved, I may send the couple to a certified sex therapist adjunctively or get consultation from a sex therapist myself. Referral or consultation issues include but are not limited to: physiological reasons that cause sexual dysfunction, lack of orgasm, difficulties with erections or ejaculation, vaginismus and chronic illness or pain.

That said, sexuality is often pivotal in couple therapy and even those who come in because they feel helpless and discouraged about their sexual intimacy may not be willing to broach it without encouragement. And then, even if they are willing, they're generally not prepared to have difficult or tender conversations without hurting each other. Therefore my first goal, even before I determine what they want and need, and whether their issues are within the scope of my expertise, is to help them talk about what it's like to talk about sexuality. I observe their body language and listen to the ease and flow of their conversation to find out if this couple can listen and speak respectfully. If so, I proceed. If not, I take time to understand their agenda around sexuality but I postpone working on it until they are more capable of skillful communication.

THERAPIST TIP

If a couple cannot regulate or unblend enough to have a respectful conversation, continue to work on their communication skills before pushing ahead with their agenda on sexuality.

When they do have the conversation about sexuality, use the feelings of your parts as a trailhead for helping your clients become comfortable with the topic.

Ask yourself:

- What do I think and believe about sexuality that might get in the way of being open and Self-led?
- When my parts get activated about my sexuality, what do they need from me?

The couple described here, Elizabeth and Jonathan, came to me because they were on the verge of a trial separation. They did not have children, they were quarreling often, and their interpretation was that they were drifting apart. During their initial interview they wanted help understanding what had happened to their sexual relationship. After several sessions of working on the harshness of their interactions, we cycled back to talking about their sexuality.

Elizabeth and Jonathan

"What is it like to broach this subject with me and with each other?" I asked, addressing them both.

"I feel uncomfortable," said Jonathan.

"Thank you for saying so," I said.

"On the other hand," he went on, "we need help."

Elizabeth nodded.

"Could you fill me in on the concern?" I asked.

"Just different needs, I think," Elizabeth said. "We're not on the same page like we used to be."

"Meaning I want to have sex more often than she does," said Jonathan.

"I don't like to be pressured," Elizabeth said.

Jonathan shrugged as if to say, *There you have it!*

"So this is clearly important and we'll get to it," I said. **"But with your permission I want to start back before today and explore your beliefs about gender roles and sexuality in general** [see *Questions for Your Clients to Answer About Sexuality* below]. **We can do that together. Or, if one or both of you prefer, I can meet with you one at a time."**

"I don't think it will be easier but if we're going to do this I think it's better for us to do it together," Elizabeth said.

"I agree," Jonathan said.

Questions for Your Clients to Answer About Sexuality

1. When and from whom did you learn about sex? How old were you?
2. How old were you when you became sexually interested?
3. Were you ever shamed about your sexuality or your body?
4. What messages about sex, your body, or the bodies of either gender did you receive from your parents or other adults in your life?
5. What messages did you receive from siblings or peers?

6. What beliefs about sex in general and your body in particular did you formulate as a result?
7. What polarizations do you have now about sex?
8. How comfortable are you talking about sex with each other?
    a. Do you have parts who stop you from talking about sex?
    b. If so, what are they worried about?
    c. What would they need from you in order to feel okay?
9. Are there specific topics about sex that make your parts uncomfortable?
    a. If so, what are they?

(My thanks to IFIO trainer Nancy Wonder for these questions.)

Many of us come out of childhood with parts who have differing beliefs and feelings about sexuality and gender roles, so I often begin by inviting people to notice any internal polarities related to these topics (Question 7 above).

"To start, would you be willing to notice your feelings and beliefs about gender and sexuality?" I asked. Handing them both a sheet of paper listing the questions above along with pens and paper, I went on: "Think about these and jot down your answers."

Once they had taken some time to write, I asked them if they would be willing to speak and listen to each other using the skillful listening and speaking skills outlined in this chapter.

After agreeing, Jonathan began: "Here's what I think. These days women want men to have a groovy feminine side but we also need a secret cowboy in our pockets and for me that's confusing."

"You experience mixed messages about your role as a man?" I said. Looking over at Elizabeth, I asked, "Are you able to listen?"

"I am," she said, "I'm interested. This cowboy is a well-kept secret!"

"Really?" Jonathan said. "Would you agree that you want me to be strong and sexy as well as sensitive?"

"Sure," Elizabeth said. "Why not?"

"Well, you tell me. When I'm decisive you act like I'm trying to push you around."

"Hmmm," said Elizabeth.

"What are you hearing?" I asked.

"I get it. He's had mixed messages all his life. And now I'm hearing that includes from me. But I think he overreacts. Yeah I do want him to be strong as well as sensitive but really it's a matter of degree and style."

"Well whatever you want," Jonathan said, "I'm not it. That's all I know. I've tried. I've given up."

"As I listen to you," I said, **"I wonder how these conversations end up at home?"**

"In a fight," Elizabeth said.

"That makes sense," I said. "And the fighting has affected your sexual relationship?"

"Yes," Jonathan said.

While Jonathan's description of his childhood illuminated the contradictory messages he got about the role of men, Elizabeth's early education about the genders proved equally confusing. Throughout her childhood she heard her mother dismiss men in general – and her father in particular – as weak and irresponsible but saw her mother defer to her father in every way. Since her father's kindness invariably exceeded his wisdom, the family finances suffered and her mother's passivity was equaled only by her verbal scorn and anger.

"Jonathan, I hear you saying that you experience Elizabeth as wanting you to be both deferential and assertive, which confuses you. Is that right?"

"Actually I'd say I wanted to be whatever Elizabeth wanted me to be and I thought I could be him but I've never succeeded. And now I don't want to succeed anymore. That guy who's always trying to please everyone is tired."

"You have a part who tried to be what he thought Elizabeth wanted and now he's tired and wants out of that role?"

Jonathan nodded.

"That's important and we'll come back to him. But first can I finish summing up so we get everything on the table?"

He nodded again.

I turned to Elizabeth, "I hear you saying that you loved your father. He was generous to a fault but at the same time he seemed to you to be strangely weak and irresponsible, and you felt angry with your mother for never interceding. Is that right?"

She nodded.

"So Jonathan has a part who feels he can't figure out how to please Elizabeth and wants to quit trying. And Elizabeth has a part who often feels disappointed with Jonathan, just as it felt disappointed with mother and father. Is that a fair summation?"

"I kind of cringe when I hear that description. But maybe it is fair," Elizabeth replied.

"How are these perspectives affecting your sexual relationship?" I asked.

"Badly," Elizabeth said.

"Feeling like a failure all the time makes me sad and angry," Jonathan said.

"Our sex life used to be fun," Elizabeth observed sadly.

According to research (Michael, Gagnon, Laumann & Kalota, 1994), half of all couples experience inhibited desire or differences in the level of their desire. In my experience of couples who seek therapy, the majority have experienced some kind of glitch in their sexual connection at some point, which they found embarrassing and mistakenly believed was unusual.

"You're not alone," I assured them. **"The beliefs and feelings we inherit can have a profound effect on our sex lives."** After describing research on the topic briefly, I said, **"If you want, I can help. But first let me invite you to think of this as a couple issue. Which means no one is to blame and you'll be a team in finding the solution."**

When I work with low desire or differences in desire, I borrow freely from Barry and Emily McCarthy's (2003) model for helping low sex couples (see The McCarthy Model below). In combination with IFIO methods like *speaking and listening, exploring needs* and *healing shamed and shaming parts,* the McCarthy's approach normalizes the couple's struggle, regulates their shame and blame cycle and helps them to experience themselves as a team who are tackling and resolving a shared challenge.

The McCarthy Model (2003)

1. Find and help parts whose extreme feeling states are killing desire: depression, anxiety, inhibition, performance anxiety and shame.
2. What gets in the way of becoming an intimate team?
3. Introduce the concept of non-demand pleasure and intimate touch without the pressure of having to achieve orgasm.
4. Talk about risking new behaviors.

As it turned out, non-demand pleasure was a crucial concept for Elizabeth and Jonathan. Although this couple came to therapy with legacy issues concerning gender roles that left them feeling disconnected and hurt – and we did address these beliefs and experiences throughout the course of their therapy – they were able to rekindle their attraction pretty quickly by taking the pressure off outcome. Using a different approach to intimacy gave them time and space to unblend from angry protectors, feel safe again, engage in touch and play and reconnect, which, in turn, garnered their courage to explore family loyalties and legacy burdens in therapy.

Summary

Communicating well involves remaining physiologically regulated during difficult conversations, which takes skill, patience and courage. Couples must have many hard conversations over the course of a lifetime. IFIO teaches individuals to make a U-turn and differentiate inside before re-turning to their partner unblended and better prepared to approach what's hard.

Sometimes couples unblend easily and with your help can begin to have different conversations rapidly. Disagreeing respectfully and staying curious about each other's needs helps protectors to soften and disarm. When the inevitable breakdowns in communication occur, withdrawing, hopeless and attacking parts no longer blend and swamp them.

Alternatively, couples with fierce protectors who have a hard time relaxing need more time and much more guidance. Slow, mindful practice in your office during which couples learn to speak for rather than from their protectors cultivates the courage and confidence they need to tackle hard conversations successfully.

Introductory Steps of IFIO

Step 1:
Listen, track cycles, invite the couple to talk about difficult issues in a different way:

- *Will you let me help you?*

Step 2:
Contract to be a parts detector:

- *I am here to help you and I will slow down or stop the interaction if parts begin to overwhelm each other.*

Step 3:
Invite the couple to negotiate who will speak and who will listen first.

Step 4:
Help the listener prepare by noticing parts who might not want to listen.

Encourage the listener to breathe and notice the heart.

Help the listener to unblend until s/he is emotionally available.

Step 5:
Coach the speaker to help her or his parts *unblend* and speak for them.

Hints about unblending:

- Encourage each partner to stay in relationship with her or his own parts:
  - *What are you noticing in your body?*
- Do not get caught in their content or in helping them find solutions.
- You may need to ask one partner to wait while you help the other to unblend and speak for parts:
  - *What is this part concerned would happen if it were to unblend and let you speak for it?*
- Validate the experience and feelings of the parts of both partners.
- Confront protectors firmly and kindly.

Step 6:
Encourage the partner who is speaking to move toward vulnerable feelings if you have permission from his or her protectors. Partners are more likely to move toward empathy when listening to or about exiles.

Step 7:
Help the listener respond from the heart. No part should be left hanging. Encourage the listener to empathize – and if that doesn't work then the therapist must offer empathy.

Questions and Requests to Use with the Listener:

- *Reflect the essence of what you just heard.* (Carl Rogers)
- *Does any of this information make sense to you? In what way?*
- *Can you respond from your heart?*

Empathic Statements from the Therapist:

- *The essence of what I'm hearing is . . .*
- *What makes perfect sense to me is . . .*

The self-disclosure that is not met with understanding, mirroring or acknowledgment is often followed by a response of deep shame, and perhaps a protective adaptive reaction (Seigel, 2003).

Step 8:
Once the speaker has received an empathic response from the listener or therapist, ask the listener to pay attention inside.

Step 9:
- If there is time, switch the roles of listener and speaker.
- Remind the couple, if necessary, about the respective jobs of the listener and speaker.
- When both are ready, ask the person who was just listening to speak for her or his parts.

5

INDIVIDUAL WORK

This chapter illustrates intrapersonal work as a healing force in couple therapy. In IFIO we facilitate deep healing work in the presence of a partner for a number of reasons, including helping the couple access Self-energy, promoting internal attachment and evoking empathy instead of judgment from the witnessing partner. Encouraging the couple to explore and be aware of how childhood affects their current behavior creates the opportunity for relational unburdenings. Also, one partner making a U-turn and doing the internal healing work of witnessing and unburdening exiles in the presence of the other partner helps the couple differentiate, which helps them to give and receive love more naturally.

Individual but Together

When one partner is blended with a part and overcome with emotion, the therapist may choose to work with that partner individually while the other one acts as a witness. This will be a paradigm shift for couple therapists who have been taught not to work with an individual during a session that involves both partners. The art of this approach is balancing relational work with individual work.

We do it for several reasons. Witnessing a partner who is accessing and attending to parts with extreme beliefs based on childhood experiences can be powerful, relieving and healing to the relationship. Therefore, if a vulnerable or highly reactive part surfaces during a session and the timing seems right the therapist may decide to get permission from both partners to focus on that part. In other words we may choose to do exile work with one partner at a time. But whoever gets to do individual work first, either in the context of the couple or an individual session, the therapist should assure them that each will eventually have the opportunity.

The Role of Childhood

Early life is the focal point of much of the individual work done within couple therapy. As described in Chapter 2, many implicit memories formed in childhood are automatically evoked in present-day intimate relationships. These memories pose the partner as a threat without any conscious awareness of why. This urge to protect based on childhood danger rather than current circumstances can happen to both partners simultaneously, causing their fear to leap and their protectors to overreact. When these ruptures go unrepaired, the relationship deteriorates to the point where ending it can look like the best option.

Fostering Internal Attachment

Research shows that behaviors such as mirroring, attuned listening, eye contact, reaching out and tender touch lead to secure bonding and attachment in relationships, whether between parent and child, or between adults (Johnson, 2004). Secure bonding is associated with success in intimate relationships (Johnson, 2004). In our view, secure attachment is also vital between parts and the Self. Attending carefully and kindly to the story of exiled parts mends the wounds created by misattunement in childhood and sets the stage for the couple to manage their old, unmet needs more skillfully.

Unburdening: Healing Lost Children

Unburdening, a term coined by Schwartz (1995), describes the IFS protocol for healing exiled parts. Parts, says Schwartz, can get stuck in the past during a traumatic life event. During these events children may feel shamed or terrified and develop negative beliefs about themselves that they experience, for various reasons, as being confirmed over time. We call these burdens. Traumatically derived beliefs are over-learned, which can make them feel unyielding. But because they lose their authority in the relationship between a part and the Self, most parts are eventually willing to let them go. This change of heart happens over time, in stages that include understanding the motivation of protectors as well as witnessing the stories of exiled parts. Once toxic beliefs have been acknowledged and released, parts embrace a kinder, more discerning and adaptive identity.

Moving from Internal Attachment to External Attachment

An ability to regulate negative affect renders the strong defenses of protective parts obsolete and permits secure attachment to the partner. Secure attachment, in turn, strengthens the individual's ability to self-regulate (Badenboch, 2008). In short, differentiated, secure bonding – inside and out – are mutually reinforcing. We use the U-turn to build secure internal attachments, setting the stage for a re-turn to the project of building secure external attachments.

Relational Unburdening

When a partner is working with the emotional pain and shame experienced in childhood, open hearted witnessing can help to release relational as well as individual burdens. This positive cycle helps us to achieve our goal of change on the inside promoting change on the outside, leading to more change on the inside, which, in turn, creates more space for change on the outside, and so on. This both/and relational model strives to promote connections inside and outside simultaneously.

Internal Work

When internal exploration is appropriate for one partner, the therapist will work directly with him while the other partner acts as a witness. Preparing both partners and gaining permission from their parts before proceeding is critical. First, check with the partner who is to do the work to ensure that he has enough Self-energy. If any parts have concerns, they will need attention before you start. Because internal work can be very tender and vulnerable, safety is key. Remind them both that you will be there to help and that the one who is doing the work has the resource of the Self inside as well.

Meanwhile, the listener must be open to the role of witness without judgment or defensiveness. If the listener does react negatively during the session, the therapist must interrupt quickly and help her to unblend. Remember to support the listener by being present and engaged through eye contact, body language and, perhaps, by verbally checking in from time to time. Staying connected with both partners is important. When this individual work is complete, the therapist focuses again on the relationship to integrate insights that have been gained and to allow the couple time to incorporate a new way of relating.

In the case below, both partners blended quickly with critical, shaming parts. When critics are relentless, I help them to be heard so they can relax. Since no real work can happen between the couple as long as shaming parts are activated, I'm less interested in which partner works first and more focused on reminding both that they have work to do. I'm also always mindful that critics protect vulnerable exiles and any work I do with a couple will eventually lead to childhood injuries. Individual work that unburdens exiles generates a feeling of internal connectedness and Self-energy, which in turn fuels the couple to do their external relational work.

The Purpose of Individual Work in Couple Therapy

- Become aware of how childhood experiences play a critical role in adult relationships.
- Foster internal attachment.
- Heal young parts who were traumatized in the past.

- Evoke empathy and understanding for the partner's inner dilemmas.
- Allow the witness to observe and take part in the partner's healing process.

Nadine and Mitch

Mitch spoke first as he gazed out the window of my office on a sunny May morning, "I'm tired of being criticized. I can never get it right for Nadine."

"Can you fill me in?" I asked Nadine.

"I know this is a lousy thing to say, but from where I sit Mitch hears everything as criticism these days. He seems oversensitive. It's like he's a different person. I don't know where this is coming from unless it's about getting laid off."

"So you have a part who's puzzled?"

"I do," she said.

"And you have this part who feels criticized by Nadine. **Does it feel criticized on the inside, too?**" I asked Mitch.

"You mean do I get angry with myself? Yes."

"**How do you feel toward the part who is angry with you?**" I asked.

"Scared."

"So another part is afraid of the angry one."

"Because he reminds me of my father."

"You were afraid of your father, weren't you?"

"He was always angry and I was always afraid of him."

I looked at Nadine. She nodded and said to Mitch, "He was a scary guy."

When one partner begins the vertical journey to childhood, the other – no longer the target of blame – is often able to feel empathic and be interested.

Turning back to Mitch, I asked, "**Can this scared part trust you?**"

"Who's me?" Mitch asked.

"Is that what you just heard inside?"

"I don't know anyone in there who can be trusted."

"Okay," I said. "Let's check with the part who doesn't trust you. Would it be willing to meet the Mitch who can be trusted?"

"It says there is no one."

"I know it feels that way. Is it the scared part?"

He nodded.

How do you feel toward it?" I asked.

"I'd like to help," he said.

"Would it let us talk to the angry part?"

"Reluctantly," Mitch said.

"Okay. If it needs help, ask it to let us know. And then ask the angry part what he does for you."

"He's really mad," Mitch said. "He's going to smash the daylights out of me."

"What would happen if he didn't smash the daylights out of you?"

"I'd screw up."

"How did he come to believe that?"

"When I was a kid I always screwed up."

"How did you know you were screwing up?"

"My father told me."

"Then no wonder this part thought you were screwing up."

"He has to get to me before anyone else does."

"Like who?"

"Nadine, my ex-boss, anyone . . ."

"Ask him to take you back to when he started doing this job," I said and Mitch began to weep. **"Is this level of feeling okay?"** I asked.

He shook his head, *No.*

"Okay," I said. Choosing a tack that would take advantage of Nadine's expression of empathy and compassion, I said, "Let's look at Nadine right now."

Even though love and support from a partner in the present will not be enough to counteract protectors who take the lead in relationships when shame permeates the inner system, a loving partner can still help regulate the fight-or-flight impulse (Porges, 2007).

"Better," he nodded to Nadine, who nodded back encouragingly.

"Okay to go back in?" I asked.

He nodded.

"Then **let's ask everyone inside to dial back on the emotion a little so you can stay with this,**" I said.

"I was so criticized as a child. It was like he hated my brothers and me. I could never get it right for him no matter how hard I tried."

"Can you see the boy in your mind's eye?"

"Yeah. He has curly hair and long, skinny legs."

"How do you feel toward him?"

"Sad."

"Is that pity or compassion?"

This is an important question. Pity reveals a part who is not comfortable and wants the feelings of the target part to change while compassion signals acceptance and is a green light to continue.

Mitch said he felt compassion and was able to stay with the sadness briefly. But then he opened his eyes and said, "I have a lot of noise going on in here."

"Say more."

"Conversation about the pointlessness of this inquiry."

"And?"

"I put all this behind me years ago. I learned to live with my father and his ways. I don't feel like revisiting it."

"You have parts who tried to put all this behind you. But when you and Nadine disagree what happens?"

"I feel like she's my father," he said.

"It doesn't have to be that way," I said. The invitation to recognize the impact of childhood on current relationships is the U-turn. **"We can help him get out of the past to live with you in the present.** Can we go back to him?"

Mitch said, "He cringes when I look at him."

"What makes sense about that?"

"He can't trust adults."

"Do you understand that?"

"Of course!"

"Can he feel you there?" I asked.

He nodded.

"Stay with him while I check with Nadine." Turning to Nadine, I said, "Have you been able to stay present while I work with Mitch?"

"Very much," Nadine said. "I know his father was a brutal man."

Turning back to Mitch, I asked, "How is your boy doing now?"

"I'm getting a lot of images of being criticized," Mitch said.

"Is there a particular time he wants you to remember?"

"Just that it went on and on."

"What did he believe about himself as a result?"

"That he was bad and deserved it. And I do have a voice in me, as you know, that agrees."

The next step was to help Mitch help this boy let go of the belief that he deserved to be shamed.

"Is he with you?" I asked, checking the connection between Mitch's Self and the boy.

"Yes."

"Does he trust that you understand?"

"He does," Mitch replied, eyes closed, tears coming down his cheeks. "I've never wanted anybody to know me. I've tried my whole life to cover this up."

Nadine leaned in and put a hand on Mitch's knee. He opened his eyes, took her hand and they looked each other in the eye. I watched until they let go and sat back again.

Mitch turned to me.

"Is he ready to get out of there?" I asked.

Mitch nodded and closed his eyes again.

I went on, "Is he ready to let go of the burdens he developed at that time?"

"Seems like that's already happening."

"Great. Stay with him. Has he unloaded the shame?"

"It's gone now."

"What does he want to invite in now that the shame is gone?"

"Laughter, lightness."

"And what was he born to do?" I asked.

"Play music," Mitch said. "He's a gifted child."

"What message do you want to give him?"

"I know what a creative kid he is and I'm so sorry all that was taken away from him. He lived in fear. I'm going to find a way to have more music and fun in our lives."

After a few moments, I invited Mitch to come back. He opened his eyes, looked around and took Nadine's proffered hand again.

"Mitch," I said, **"can the boy look out through your eyes at Nadine, feel her hand, see her tenderness?"**

"Yes he can."

"What's that like?" I asked.

"He likes it," Mitch said.

"Is there anything he wants to say to Nadine or have you say for him?" I asked.

"Thanks for being here for him – for us."

"I love this boy," Nadine replied. "I want him to know that."

This was a lovely example of a *relational unburdening*. As Mitch witnessed and offered love to his terrorized child, Nadine's entire system softened, allowing her to be progressively more available to the boy and Mitch. In turn, the child felt bathed in the love he desperately needed, inside and out. Inner and outer attunement of this kind shifts implicit ways of knowing – our old beliefs and memories – over to explicit awareness, correcting relational expectations by contradicting them. Often the effect is lasting (Ecker, 2012).

THERAPIST TIP

- Check your own state at the outset of a session.
- Access Self-energy with your breath and your body.
- Stay attuned and connected internally as well as with your clients.

Intrapersonal Work in the Presence of a Partner[1]

The ongoing work that Nadine and Mitch did with me after this session included more self-exploration, unburdening of young exiles and the practice of speaking for parts and listening from the Self so they could hear their requests as requests. The more contact they had with their exiles, the more they recognized each other as frustrated partners rather than as the one who *wounds* from the past or the longed for *redeemer* of the present.

THERAPIST TIP

- Proceed with the internal work of one client only when the witnessing partner can stay unblended.
- Trust your intuition.
- Remember you are working in a triad not a dyad. To deepen the work and facilitate *relational unburdening* it is optimal for the witnessing partner to stay present and engaged.
- Therefore, the therapist must remain connected and attuned to both partners, even while working intensely with one. This can be done by making eye contact or by taking a moment to check in with the witnessing partner:
  - *Can you stay open and curious with me while your partner is working with this part?*
- Safety is imperative for both partners.

Summary

Doing individual work in couple therapy is unconventional but, in our experience, healing. In IFIO our job is to gently and respectfully facilitate internal attachment work, developing a compassionate dialogue between the client and his vulnerable, injured parts while at the same time supporting the partner to witness this work with presence and compassion. This dual focus on vulnerability summons the couple's Self-energy and conjures love for their exiles, inside and out.

The Steps of Individual Work

Step 1:
- Contract with the couple for one partner to do individual work with an internal focus.

Step 2:
- Help the person who will be witnessing to unblend and feel available.
- Remind the couple you will be checking in with them frequently.

Step 3:
- Gently and respectfully facilitate internal attachment work, developing compassionate dialogue between the client and her wounded exile(s).
- Bring mindful attention to the protective system to maintain safety and neural regulation.

Step 4:
- Heal the exile by the Self witnessing and helping the exile to unburden shame.

Step 5:
- When possible, support the interpersonal connection between partners by acknowledging and introducing young parts to the witnessing partner.

NOTE

1 The individual work described in this chapter follows the protocol of IFS therapy. For more information, read the book *Internal Family Systems Therapy* by Richard Schwartz.

6

COUNTERTRANSFERENCE IN COUPLE THERAPY

In this chapter we talk about a key aspect of our work, the role of the therapist and our view of countertransference. Couple therapists must navigate some extremely complex situations. To do so effectively, we look inward first, developing and maintaining solid internal connections and discovering what's happening with our parts when we feel stuck. Here we offer some questions that we ask to keep sessions Self-led. In IFIO (as in IFS) we aim to bring the same curiosity, care and compassion to our parts that we guide our clients to bring to their parts. To be effective we must first and foremost practice what we preach.

The Therapist's U-turn

Like therapists working in any other model, IFIO therapists experience transference and countertransference. That is, our clients evoke our parts. Recognizing that transference and countertransference form continual cycles of action and reaction – at times fostering a sense of closeness and connection, at other times a feeling of distress – therapists who work with couples must learn to pay attention to their parts.

In the service of learning to allow, accept and work directly with whatever arises in the therapy office we encourage both client and therapist to look inward to understand the feelings of parts. The angry, defensive, grandiose, vulnerable and shamed parts of our clients – or us – have great power to evoke other people's protectors. Even the most skilled therapist can blend with an exile and feel overwhelmed, freeze, feel anxious, afraid or intimidated; or we may blend with a protector and have the impulse to take sides, express anger or withdraw. We may try to control one partner or the other, and we may also have parts who question our ability to be helpful or wish to defend us from injury. All of this is common and to be expected. A large part of our job is noticing and caring for our own parts.

THERAPIST TIP

Make a habit of asking yourself these questions:

- *Is my body relaxed, my nervous system regulated?*
- *If I'm triggered, who am I reminded of?*
- *What do I feel as I listen to this couple?*
- *Am I leaning toward one partner over the other?*
- *Do I feel friendly toward their protectors?*
- *Does one partner scare or intimidate me?*
- *Will my parts hold onto their views and quiet down so I can hear the couple?*

As we explore, understand and attend inside, our inner conversations, judgments and responses to clients deserve respect and careful attention – this is important information about us and sometimes about the couple. Being in relationship with our parts helps us access more inner resources, and knowing our parts also tells us what about us may be stalling the process. We believe that attending to the feelings and beliefs of our parts gives us the opportunity to develop a sustainable therapeutic alliance so that sessions can be collaborative and empowering.

The Embodied Therapist

Grounding physically and mentally before beginning a session is a good idea. The more physically attuned we are, the faster we can return to the Self when parts get energized. Once parts begin to trust and differentiate internally, their striving and tension tend to give way to a feeling of relaxation and liveliness, signaling that the body is more available as a vehicle for Self-energy (McConnell, 2013).

In IFIO we teach therapists to be aware of their bodies as a way to identify parts in the body who may be interfering with the work. People ground themselves in their body in many ways, including breathing, relaxing and sending energy to areas of tension. The more attuned we are to the body, the more quickly we can return to the Self when parts begin to blend.

Working with Triangles

Because adding a third helps to alleviate tensions in a dyad, the relational triangle has long been of interest to clinicians who work with systems. More differentiated individuals who either have a history of healthier, more supportive triangles or more skill with negotiating differences will have less need to incorporate a third into their dyads.

Noting that couple therapy is inherently triangular, IFIO trainer Michele Bograd brought Bowen's family systems concept of the triangulated therapist to IFIO (Bowen, 1978). Couples come to therapy as a dyad seeking stabilization due to unresolved tension. Even though adding a third does nothing to resolve their issues, spreading that tension can help to stabilize their system. Think of adding a third leg under a tabletop. The caveat is that this stabilization depends on the steadiness and strength of the third leg. Bowen (1978) observed that when participants around the triangle compete for recognition and resource, they all get locked into an inherently weak position. At this point the work will come to a halt. In contrast, if one member of the triangle remains calm and emotionally connected with the other two, calm is likely to prevail.

Since blended parts reach for the most habitual – not the most effective – coping strategy in response to danger, Bograd suggests that we therapists want to become knowledgeable about our personal position in important early triangles. Awareness of the roles our parts took in times of stress helps us be alert to blending that can destabilize the therapeutic triangle rather than helping to calm the couple.

For example, some couples will present in therapy hoping that the therapist will help to change the other person's behavior. And either partner may have parts who are highly skilled at triangulating a third person into their conflict. Depending on the therapist's history as it relates to the content of this conversation or the role played during conflict in childhood, the therapist may get recruited to lean one way or the other. Doing so, however, immediately destabilizes the triangle and the therapist finds herself unwittingly allied with one partner against the other.

THERAPIST TIP

Think of a difficult clinical situation involving a couple and take a moment to ask yourself the following questions:

- *What is my knee-jerk reaction?*
- *Where do I feel comfortable in this triangle?*
- *Is this feeling familiar from childhood?*
- *What role did my parts play in the triangles in my family of origin (for example, mediator, scapegoat, protector)?*
- *Are there times when I assume this role with couples in my office?*

(My thanks to Michele Bograd, who developed these questions.)

How to Work with Countertransference

Carl Rogers (1951) believed that being genuine, real and self-aware were key ingredients of optimal growth and change, meaning that these behaviors help the client and therapist to experience emotional synchrony. With compassion, curiosity, clarity and an open heart we connect with clients, help them to regulate aroused parts and support them in unblending. Most important, we can see the wounded exiles behind protectors and find the courage to kindly yet firmly challenge them, both understanding and interrupting harmful interactions.

Speaking for your parts in the role of therapist can be a supportive intervention. For instance, when working with a client who has a self-hating part, I may express my sadness. On occasion I will speak on behalf of a part who resonates with it. In my experience, self-revealing interactions that invite the client to see me as a human being who has parts who struggle and a Self who connects and heals can contribute to a trusting relationship.

The following example illustrates an interaction I had with my client, Michael, as he struggled with a part who would periodically declare "I'm out of here" to his partner.

"I understand these parts, Michael," I said. "I, too, have a part who can pull me away from my partner when I feel threatened. I understand parts who do that are very protective." Michael nodded as I continued. "I also know this part's behavior is painful for my partner."

"Well at least the impulse makes sense to you," he said.

"Yes, it does. And there is another way to feel safe if you're interested."

In IFIO we highlight a few concerns related to countertransference, including fear of anger and conflict, discomfort with certain content (for example, affairs, sexuality, addiction and class, race or power differences), and the ubiquitous inner critic, who shames in an attempt to prevent feelings of shame and failure. Often the critic has absolutely no perspective on the paradox or futility of this behavior and compounds the problem by pouncing internally when the therapist feels overwhelmed, frozen or stuck. The following case example illustrates when and how therapists can help their critics.

Taming the Dragon: Loving Your Inner Critic

"I don't want to say anything that would shame them," Zoe explained to me, her supervisor.

"How would you shame them?" I asked.

"I actually want to let them have it and tell them that the way they're talking to each other is childish, stupid and causes more harm than good," Zoe said.

Zoe was correct that this couple's behavior was not productive but she was also unable to intervene skillfully because a part who felt dysregulated by the couple was blended with her.

"Perhaps there's wisdom to that inclination," I said. "I'm curious about the part who feels this way. Can we take a moment to notice it?" I asked.

"It's like major anxiety here in my stomach."

"Okay to focus on that?" I asked. Trusting that Zoe already had experience with negotiating this terrain, I was quiet.

"Ugh!" she said. "I know what this reminds me of. My parents fought when I was young. I tried to mediate, unsuccessfully of course. This feels embarrassing."

"Say more."

"I'm embarrassed that I fell so easily into the same role working with couples after all these years of education and work!"

"A critic dressing you down?" I asked.

"Yep."

"Shall we help it?" I asked.

The inner critic often deploys first with therapists, as with clients. Our protective parts judge our performance because they believe, *The more we shame you, the better you will be and the better you will do.* If we don't notice and help them to be less extreme, their relentless input can be paralyzing.

"Oh god. This part thinks I should be way better at this by now," Zoe said. "It's frantic about my reputation."

"What does it want for you?"

"It says it just wants me to be a decent therapist."

"Anything you want to say to it?"

"This approach doesn't help."

"How does it respond?"

"Nothing else works!"

"Where did this part learn that criticizing would improve you?"

Zoe paused. "I had a learning disability and I was humiliated in front of other kids. But I kept trying because I was terrified about failing and getting in trouble. My family is all about performance and ambition."

"So what does it think criticizing you will do for you?"

"Fix me up. Make me into the person I was supposed to be. It jumps all over me if I make a mistake."

"How do you feel toward it?" I asked.

"Oh, I know it's been a hard working friend for many years. I'd like to help it retire with dignity," Zoe smiled. "But it doesn't believe that's an option."

"Do you have parts who feel hopeless about this critic?" I asked.

"Definitely," she replied.

"How long has it been around?"

"I don't know exactly. But I do know that I was made to stand up in class while teachers berated me for this, that and the other thing. I think this critic picked up where my teachers left off."

"How do you feel toward it as you remember grade school?"

"Pretty sad. Sad for the school girl who felt like a failure and sad that other parts started criticizing her, thinking it would motivate her to stay ahead of the curve."

Zoe realized that the relationship between the girl who felt like a failure and the critic who was trying to help her succeed were most active during her work with certain clients, which gave her more insight into her history. She began to greet this critic with the kindness due an earnest, well-meaning child, and continued to work with it as the exile it protected got out of the cross-fire during sessions, allowing her to take the lead with Self-energy.

Handling Difficult Content

Couple therapists can be faced with extreme parts in clients and also extreme subject matter. When the IFIO therapist remains in connection with his parts from a Self-led place, clients are more likely to trust that he can be open and available, regardless of the subject matter. Difficult content includes affairs, pornography addiction, parenting, power differences, chronic and relentless self-criticism and mental or physical health issues, to name a few. If a topic evokes strong beliefs in the therapist, or taps into his history or current relationship dilemmas, remaining in a state of Self-led awareness will not be easy. Below is another example from my supervisory experience with a therapist whose parts got activated by infidelity.

"What a liar!" Aram said. "This woman has been coming to therapy and still sleeping with another guy!"

"What's coming up for you right now?" I asked.

"Plain and simple: she's a liar and a cheat."

"And what does that mean to you?" I persisted.

"I can't work with them if she's still having the affair."

"Say more," I said.

Aram hesitated. "Well all the literature about affairs..." his voice trailed off.

"I think I understand your feelings," I said. "And I know that many therapists have parts who feel strongly about infidelity. But before I decide to terminate with a client, I always listen to my reactive parts. Want to try?"

"Yeah, yeah, yeah, I get it," Aram replied. "Let's see! I had a strong reaction, didn't I?"

"Who's that?" I asked.

"An angry, judgmental part."

"Check with it," I said.

"I have a knot in my stomach," putting his hand on his belly.

Since sensations often lead to hidden material, I said, "Stay with that, if it's okay."

"My dad had affairs," he reported. "And I hated him for it. I knew he was doing it but my mother only suspected. And I've been cheated on. I can't tolerate this behavior in my office."

"That makes sense," I said. "And what else does the part say?"

"It's too painful. It's irreparable and the offender will never take responsibility. Relationships with people who act like that are not worth the effort."

"Your dad and your boyfriend never took responsibility?" I asked.

"That's right. Just like this guy in my office, I had to deal with it alone."

We invite parts who are caught in the crossfire between clients because of their own experience to tell their stories and get help unburdening their black and white, all-or-nothing perspective. It made all the sense in the world that this issue would unseat Aram when these parts were blended with him. He could only make a conscious, Self-led decision about working with this couple if he helped his judgmental protector and his injured exile. We make the same invitation to ourselves that we make to our clients. Inner work leads to Self-led choices.

Therapist, Love Your Parts!

In IFIO we handle countertransference by teaching therapists to practice the U-turn so that feelings and reactivity are an opportunity to love both hard working and injured parts, and to bring Self-leadership and presence to the therapeutic relationship. Schwartz (2013) has a saying: *Self heals.* In support of this claim, research on mindfulness and self-compassion (Neff, 2011) concludes that compassion and self-forgiveness have an internal healing effect and also help us to be more loving with others.

Summary

Although countertransference may inform us about our clients' parts, we attend to our reactions first as information about our parts. Therapists, like clients, have parts who suffer and these parts are liable to get caught in the cross-fire of a couple in con-flict. As we teach our clients to bring kindness and attention to their parts, we do the same, befriending all of who we are and bearing witness to what we have been through. The practice of self-compassion makes it possible to take responsibility for our actions (Neff, 2011).

7

NEGOTIATING NEEDS

In this chapter we cover the vital issue of how to help couples negotiate emotional needs using the IFIO tools. Many people are confused about what they need and clumsy at asking to have a need met. The IFIO approach guides and supports couples in understanding how they project childhood injury into current relationships and helps them identify the true needs underlying their frustration and anger. We also teach them to make requests that invite rather than threaten the partner into meeting those needs. And, not least, we help each partner to sustain a loving relationship with her own parts so when the partner is not available no part is left feeling alone.

True Need

Needs that we all share include the need to feel recognized, understood and loved. We need emotional security, connection and the felt knowledge that we are not alone (Siegal, 2003). In my experience, many people feel ashamed of needs, struggle to acknowledge them and don't know how to incentivize an intimate partner to meet them. Early in a relationship, this negotiation often seems easy because new lovers tend to be emotionally available without being asked. But as time goes on and a couple goes through ruptures, miscommunications and moments of misattunement – not to mention the demands of daily life – protections build, attentiveness falls away and need can seem to be a dangerous vulnerability.

When the need for love and connection evokes feelings of loneliness, sadness, fear, longing, and shame we are likely to find that we're blended with an exile. When we launch into ineffective behaviors geared to cover wounded exiles like attacking or withdrawing, we are, in contrast, blended with protectors. For an intimate partnership to be viable, emotional needs must be met. Protectors, as we see throughout the examples in this book, are not effective mediators of need. Relationship building is not their bailiwick; instead their mission is to prevent reenactments of the past, or sometimes simply to prevent the past. Of course, we know that they don't know how to do the former and the latter is impossible.

The IFIO approach to couple therapy guides and supports couples in learning how to speak for parts and make requests that invite rather than threaten their partners into responding. Once they are able to negotiate with more skill, protectors are less likely to attack or withdraw, which in turn allows the therapy to promote a more optimal and stable sense of connectedness and differentiation inside and out. Although behavioral change takes time, with practice, patience and repetition couples can change (Lind-Kyle, 2009). In my experience, the incentive to stick with the process derives largely from the U-turn, which makes couples mindful of how they are projecting childhood injury and helps them to discover the true need underlying their frustration and anger.

Fleshing It Out

The following case illustrates six steps that help a couple identify and meet emotional needs. **First**, we identify the issues. **Second**, and often most time consuming, we identify the couple's fight (or collapse) cycle. **Third**, we validate and unblend frustrated or angry protectors. **Fourth**, we invite one partner at a time to do a U-turn, exploring childhood events that illuminate the need beneath the anger. **Fifth**, we help the client return to her partner and speak for what she learned. **Sixth**, we teach the client to ask the partner to meet a need in the here and now.

Finding and Meeting Emotional Needs

1. Identify the issues.
2. Identify the couple's fight (or collapse) cycle.
3. Validate and unblend frustrated or angry protectors.
4. Invite one partner at a time to do a U-turn and explore childhood events to understand the needs beneath the anger.
5. Help the client re-turn to the partner and speak for what she learned.
6. Teach the client how to ask to have a need met in the here and now.

Step One: Identify the Issues

Tom and Isabel

"I've brought him to therapy so he can learn about his feelings," Isabel announced after a couple of sessions.

This kind of opening is common in couple therapy. One partner invites the other to counseling hoping the partner will agree to have his emotional life examined. However, coming from a desperate part, this invitation is usually experienced by the partner as a demand.

"So Tom," I said, turning to Isabel's husband, "when Isabel says she wants you to share your feelings, what does that mean to you?"

"Honestly ... I don't really feel much," he replied.

"I hear you," I said. **"What are you saying to yourself about you or Isabel right now?"**

He paused for a moment, "Honestly?"

"Honestly," I said.

"I have no idea what she wants from me. I'm not a feeler or a talker. I do things. Half the time I don't know what she's asking for. I try to give her what she wants, but evidently I don't know how."

"You don't try," said Isabel, her voice barely audible.

"Isabel," I said, turning toward her, "**what's happening right now**, in this moment, for you?"

"I'm frustrated."

"I hear that," I responded gently. **"What's underneath your frustration?"**

Isabel stared out the window and shifted her body toward me and away from Tom.

"I'm lonely," she said. "I have been for a long time. I feel hopeless... like our relationship will always be... disconnected."

"Tom," I said, **"I'm curious. What are you hearing?"**

"I'm used to her being angry." He was quiet for a moment. "I didn't know she felt hopeless."

"What's it like to hear that Isabel has a hopeless part?" I inquired, taking the opportunity to introduce parts language.

"Uncomfortable," he said.

"What does this uncomfortable part of you want to say to Isabel?"

"I want you to be happy. I don't want you to feel hopeless," he said, looking at her. "I know you want something different from me. I just don't know how to do it."

"I don't believe you!" Isabel shot back.

Tom looked defeated.

"Again, **what just happened**?" I asked Isabel.

"I'm not going to let him off that easily," she said, looking defiant.

THERAPIST TIP

When one partner is vulnerable and the other attacks:

- Validate the (exile) vulnerability that drives the attack.
- And be clear, firm and kind about helping the attacking part to unblend.

Step Two: Identify the Couple's Fight (or Collapse) Cycle

Isabel was angry after years of feeling little connection with her husband. A significant amount of relational injury over many years takes time to untangle and repair. A moment of vulnerability from Tom, albeit lacking an articulation of his feelings, did not erase her years of disappointment.

"Your anger makes sense," I said. "You're asking for something important and meaningful and you have a part who is angry about having waited so many years. Am I right?"

"Yes," Isabel replied.

**Step Three: Validate and Unblend Frustrated or
Angry Protectors**

"And if this part didn't go after Tom, what is it afraid would happen?"

"He'll stay complacent!" she said.

"And then?"

"Our life will go on like this! Nothing would be different, nothing would ever change."

In this model we believe that a protector like Isabel's is making a desperate bid for connection, so we validate its intention over and over without condoning its behavior.

"This angry part is up to something it believes will be good for you and maybe good for your relationship, too, is that right?"

"I guess you could say that."

"And it believes the only way to keep Tom engaged is to stay angry even when he begins to do the very thing you asked for, which is to start becoming aware of feelings?" I asked.

"When you put it that way it sounds like I'm nuts. But he never changes!" Isabel said, still too blended with her angry part to experience Tom's concern as progress.

"Trying to get another person to change is hard work," I said to both of them. "From where I sit, this pattern you're in now looks frustrating and painful, and I do believe there's another way. **I would like to help you learn to negotiate more effectively so that you can both get what you need."**

"I'm always asking for what I need," said Isabel.

"I believe you," I said. "From what I hear, both of you have parts who make requests – but the requests are cloaked in criticism. **I can teach you how to let you make requests more effectively."**

"That's what we're here for," Tom said.

I looked at him and then her, waiting for her response. She said nothing.

"Would you be willing to find out more about your part who is so frustrated?" I finally asked her.

"I can feel it all over my body," she said.

"Focus on it and we'll let it be here with you for a moment without wishing it away," I said. After a moment, I asked "How do you feel toward it?"

"I understand it."

"Let it know what you understand and see if there's more."

After giving Isabel a few more moments to be with the part, I continued: "What's it like for this part to be understood by you?"

"Good."

"What is it afraid will happen if it doesn't stay angry?"

"He'll never get it."

"And what does this part want Tom to get?"

"That I don't want to feel alone. I want him to understand me, listen to me, care about my feelings, understand his own feelings."

"How does Tom respond to this part?"

"He resists," she said.

"Can you step back to observe the cycle between you and Tom and what happens when your anger and his resistance get into a stand off?"

"We're miserable," she reported.

"Is your angry part aware of this?"

"It doesn't care," she said. "Nothing else works."

"That's right, nothing else has worked," I agreed. "And, again, **if it were to stop doing what it does, what is it afraid would happen to you?**"

"I'll be alone."

Step Four: Find the Childhood Predicament

"Is your anger protecting another part?" I asked Isabel.

"There is a lonely little girl in there," she said after a moment, referring to the wounded exile who was motivating her angry protector.

"How do you feel toward her?"

"Sad."

"Sad with your heart open to her?" I asked

"Yes," Isabel replied.

"And how does she respond?"

"She's still sad."

"Yes she is. What does she want you to know about her lonely sadness?"

"She was left alone all the time. No one was there. Not emotionally anyway."

"Does she feel you here with her now?"

"Yes."

"What does she need from you?"

"She wants me to listen."

"Okay with you?"

Isabel opened her eyes and said, "But I want Tom to do this. I always have to take care of myself!"

While jarring, this response from an alarmed protector is common, especially for individuals who were neglected in childhood. The best strategy is to normalize and validate the need for loving attention.

"Of course you want Tom to do this," I said. "And that's where we're headed. But first let's introduce this little girl to you."

"Why?"

"Because while Tom can't always be there for her, you can. So she needs both of you."

Isabel closed her eyes again and was silent for a moment. "I should never have been left alone!" she said suddenly, tears welling up.

Noticing that she was speaking *from* rather than *for* the little girl now, I responded, "That's right. Do you get that, Isabel? She should never have been left alone. She didn't deserve to be treated that way – no child does."

"She thought she was unlovable."

I glanced at Tom, who nodded, clearly engaged. Returning to Isabel, I asked "And what is true about this child?"

"She's beautiful, lively! She's a sweet kid."

"Does she hear you?"

"This is sad. She wonders where I've been."

"What do you say to her?" I asked.

"I didn't mean to leave you alone. I'm here now."

"And how does she respond?"

"She's glad but she doesn't trust me."

"What does she need from you right now?"

"She doesn't want me to leave."

"She wants to stay with you. Is that okay with you? Then let her know. And tell her that we'll return to help her."

"Okay," Isabel reported.

"Is it okay if I ask you something now about another part?"

"Yes."

"What's the relationship between this little girl and the angry part?"

"He says he protects her."

"What's he doing now?"

"He's watching."

"All those years of feeling isolated and alone, no wonder he got angry on her behalf. We can come back to him, too," I said. "But right now, is it okay to return to Tom?"

Step Five: Re-turning to the Partner with Insight

Isabel opened her eyes and looked at Tom.

"I heard you," he said. After a pause, he added, "I'm sorry. I know I disappear. But it's not that I intend to leave you alone."

I said to Isabel, "How is it for you when Tom listens?"

"Better," she replied.

Step Six: Making a Request

Before encouraging a client to become more vulnerable by making a request, assess whether she has enough Self-energy to tolerate *no* and help her to unblend and take care of young parts by focusing inside and speaking for the need. This way if the partner's answer is no, or the partner is only open to granting a portion of the request, the vulnerable part (the part with the need) is already in relationship to the client's Self and has some protection against re-injury.

"Do you have a request for Tom right now?" I asked Isabel.

"Would you walk the dog with me after dinner tonight?" she said.

He smiled wryly, "*That* I can do."

The next step after this would be Tom working with the parts who shut him down.

A Choice in Every Moment©

Several years ago I designed an exercise (based on an exercise developed in 1995 by Kate and Joel Feldman for couples who attend their workshops) to explore the emotional needs beneath anger and to make requests skillfully. I call it *A Choice in Every Moment* (see box below). This exercise is geared to help clients *slow down and use a number of steps to maximize their sense of choice when responding to a partner.* They include *accessing the frustrated part; recognizing repetitive, patterned interactions; exploring childhood history to locate the exile who fuels the behavior; and finally listening for the need of the exile from the Self.*

My goal with *A Choice in Every Moment* is to slow clients down so they can explore and understand the longings and core emotional needs that were exiled in childhood. Once people tune in to the original experience of being wounded and understand the way in which a core need was left unmet due to this injury, they are more tolerant and compassionate toward the present needs of their parts. This, in turn, helps them to unblend and make requests more skillfully, from the Self rather than from protective parts. Perhaps most important, when people are in a Self-led relationship with their parts, they are far more likely to see and exercise choice in the way they respond, regardless of whether the partner is available.

THERAPIST TIP

Do the following exercise yourself before you do it with a couple. Integrate the material from the inside out by exploring your needs. I usually offer this as a guided meditation and then have clients answer the questions below in writing before having them return to talk about the experience as a couple.

A Choice in Every Moment©

- Focusing your attention on your anger or frustration: What do you notice? What do you hear?
- What is your most automatic response when you feel frustrated?
  - For example, you feel controlling, angry, impatient, manipulative, submissive, analyzing...
  - Ask yourself who is reacting, and notice that part.
- What response does your reaction typically elicit from your partner?
- What happens *inside you* when your partner responds this way?
  - For example, you feel angry, sad, happy, excited, anxious...

- What do you notice about this cycle of action and coun-teraction between your protectors and your partner's protectors?
- If you listen closely to your frustrated protector, can you sense the vulnerable part (the exile) underneath?
  - What do you see, feel or sense about the exile?
  - What childhood incident or pattern of interaction injured this part?
  - What did this part need from a caregiver at the time that it didn't get?
  - Ask if you can provide at least a little of that right now.
- What do you need from your partner in relation to this part or issue?
- Now bring the *U-turn* to a *re-turn* and try speaking for these parts with your partner.
  - Can you make a request from your Self for something right now?

Summary

We view anger and frustration as clues to the needs of these individuals to be seen, heard and known that were not met in childhood, and we help them swim beneath the surface to see how those needs drive their protectors. If the couple is wedded to the view that self-care undermines their pledge to care for each other, they can be surprised when we assert that self-care is as relationally essential as mutual generosity and that the Self is a source of love when the partner is unavailable. We further assert that it's okay to ask the partner to meet a need and pos-sible to do so with skill. And then we help them practice.

8

YOU, ME, WE?

NEGOTIATING CORRESPONDING NEEDS THAT CONFLICT

In this chapter we address the question of how to handle corresponding but conflicting needs, a phenomenon all couples must navigate. We normalize the experience and assert that they can learn to negotiate conflicting needs. Our goal is to help the couple recognize that they both have valid needs and that, once again, the experience of being shamed for having needs in childhood has inhibited them from negotiating skillfully.

Who First?

Getting needs met generally involves two separate but related concerns: What do we do if our partner is not available to give us what we need exactly when we want it? Whose needs take precedence when our needs conflict? Our goal is to help couples negotiate these questions without bitter power struggles.

We teach clients that exiles who look for redemption from painful childhood experiences can get what they need from the Self first and a partner second (Schwartz, 2008). In my experience, once individuals have established a secure, differentiated attachment between their parts and Self, they focus less on the other person needing to change, they feel more present and are more available to the needs of others without feeling overwhelmed or resentful. Equally, they can learn to set gentle boundaries when their own needs take precedence. I remind couples that imbalance in this negotiation (for example, one person's needs are always the priority) diminishes the relationship and will be part of the work in therapy.

Vera and Peter

"What's the issue you want to work on today?" I asked.

"Go ahead," said Vera, eyeing Peter.

"I feel like I'm constantly chasing Vera, trying to get her to spend more time with me," Peter said. "She never sits still. She's always on the computer or the phone. I'm not a priority anymore ... at least not like I used to be. If it weren't for me, we probably wouldn't spend any time together, go on vacation, or even have sex!"

I glanced at Vera, inviting her to fill in.

"Peter," Vera said, "I am the breadwinner. I work all the time. When I get home I'm exhausted. The kids need me, you need me and all I want is a little down time to get my head together."

This cycle, too, is common in couples. Regardless of the content of the argument, I begin by helping them understand the underlying nature of their conflict.

"So, Peter, **you're chasing Vera for connection? Would you tell me how you do that**?"

"I am the asker," Peter said. "I ask and ask and ask. Eventually I get frustrated and then I'm sure my asking has an edge to it."

As we see here, one person is often focused on being closer while the other is demanding space. The partner who seeks more intimacy may be seen as *needy* by the other, while the distancing partner is more likely to be seen as shut down. In my experience, those who understand their desire for ample individual space as a need for independence are generally avoidant, while those who seek to be closer often fear being alone. In either case, as they search for healthy differentiation both may feel shame about their particular role.

Noting Vera's tight mouth and crossed arms, I spoke to her directly. **"What's happening?"**

"Peter is making it sound like I don't do anything to make this relationship work."

"So," I asked kindly, "what you just heard is that Peter believes you don't do anything?"

Peter shook his head and sighed. "That's not what I said. This is the problem. Vera is so sensitive and hears everything as criticism. There's no point in even trying to talk."

"No," said Vera. "You don't hear yourself and you don't take any responsibility for the way you talk to me!"

"Okay," I said to them. "**Let's slow down and see if I understand.** Peter, you have a part who feels you don't have enough quality time with Vera. That part is frustrated when Vera feels criticized by you asking for more of her time. Vera, you work a lot. Your part who needs downtime feels blamed by Peter when he wants to spend more time with you. Am I getting it?"

"Yes," they agreed.

"The way I see it, I can't get it right no matter how I try." Vera looked at Peter. "Nothing I do satisfies you."

I turned to Vera, "Would you be willing to stay with the part who just said, *I can't get it right* for a moment?"

"I'm exhausted," Vera replied. "I'm on guard all the time."

"**So which part needs your attention first**, the one who *can't get it right*, the one who's *exhausted*, or the one who's *on guard all the time?*"

"The one who's on guard."

"**How do you feel toward it?**"

"Oh I know it well!"

"And how do you feel toward it?"

"Grateful."

"**Who does it protect?**"

"When I was a kid, my father had to be the center of attention all the time. I mean all the time. It was embarrassing. My mother secretly hated him and my brothers all acted crazy. I just learned to disappear. Being alone was better than being around them."

"So this part guards a girl who felt she had no place in her family and learned to disappear because her father's needs sucked up all the oxygen?"

"That's me. This guard doesn't like needy people."

"So does it make sense to you that it would be wary of Peter's needs?"

"Yeah," Vera said after a beat.

I turned to Peter, "And your family?"

"I was one of seven children. Truthfully, I was either trying to get noticed or waiting for the opportunity to try to get noticed."

"If there was a way to negotiate needs between the two of you with less fear of either being trampled or abandoned, would you be up for learning how?"

They nodded.

"Okay. I can help you."

Next Session

Peter began the following session: "I asked for something this week and it didn't go well."

"Did your parts clash?" I asked.

"Yes," said Vera.

"Let's do it over. First tell me what happened, then we'll unpack it, maybe get to know some parts who got reactive and try again," I offered.

"When Vera got home from work I asked if she would spend time with me and the kids before listening to her voicemail or checking her email," Peter reported. "I think I did pretty well in the asking."

"Okay," Vera said. "Sounds reasonable but he knows I can't do that and he knows why. So it was a set up."

"What did you feel?" I asked her.

"Angry. And I know I was harsh."

"And what was the hope of your angry part?" I asked.

"To set a boundary. Again!"

"What was the most important thing for the angry part about setting that boundary in that way?"

"To make him get it."

"And **what happened?**"

"He felt injured, of course."

"I'd like to help you set boundaries and feel comfortable saying no to Peter in a way that doesn't rupture your connection."

"Sounds nice," Vera said with an edge of sarcasm.

"But you don't believe it's possible? That's understandable. Are you willing to try anyway? Let's go back to the moment when you felt angry."

Vera closed her eyes and nodded slightly.

"Focus on your body. What do you notice?"

"Tightening in my chest," she said.

"Ask the part in your chest to be with you for a moment without taking you over," I said. "Is it willing?"

She nodded.

"Then try leaning into that sensation so it can give you information," I said.

"It's all about you, it's all about you!" Vera burst out.

"Your father?" I asked gently.

"Yes."

"Is this part mistaking Peter for your father?" I asked. **"Would it be willing to look at Peter right now through your eyes?"**

Vera opened her eyes and looked at Peter intently.

"Who does it see?" I asked.

"I see my husband," she said.

"We don't want to hurt you," Peter smiled. "We like you. We just want to spend time with you."

Vera's eyes filled with tears. "Thank you for saying that."

After a moment, I said, **"And it's okay to say no. You can ask for what you need, too."**

"That's hard for me," Vera said.

"I know. Can I help? **Let's go back to the angry part who sets boundaries. What would happen if it relaxed?"**

"I'd be overwhelmed by everyone's needs. I'm never alone unless I get tough about it."

"Would this one who gets tough be willing to let *you* help the one who gets overwhelmed?"

"Okay."

After I helped Vera to unblend from her protectors and get curious about the overwhelmed part, she said, "When I'm on my way home in the car after being pulled in a million directions all day, I panic. I just dread that feeling of being sucked in and

pushed under by everyone's demands the minute I walk through
the door. It's like a riptide. I'm seeing now that going straight to
the phone and computer is a way to handle those feelings. I'm
going to go out on a limb and tell the truth here – I don't need
to keep working when I get home."

"What does this panicked part need from you?"

"Protection."

"How do you feel toward it?"

"I get it. I see how over-stimulated this part is by my job and
how incapable it feels when the kids are tired and needy. I want
to take care of it."

"How does it respond?"

"It feels a little hopeless, like it's bad and has ruined my life."

"Is some other part telling it that?"

"Yeah I think so."

"Ask the other part if saying that works."

"You mean criticizing? No."

**"So would it be willing to let you help the one who gets
overwhelmed?"**

"It says okay but it better work."

"I guess threats are an old habit for this part? Well that's
okay. **It doesn't have to believe in this new way of doing things
but if it wants results it does have to give you the chance to try
without interrupting.** Is it willing?"

"Yes."

"It will benefit, too. This is for everyone."

"Okay."

"How do you feel toward the overwhelmed part now?"

"I can see her. She's little. No wonder she feels overwhelmed!"

**"Does she know that you can take care of work and the kids
and your relationship with Peter?"**

"She's surprised to hear you say that."

"Because...?"

Vera shook her head slowly. "She's been responsible for my
life for a long time. I really didn't know! I'm telling her how
sorry I am. I didn't mean for it to be that way."

"Ask her who she protects."

Vera closed her eyes and was quiet but looked puzzled.

"Don't censor – what do you get?"

"I got this flash of a baby," she said. "What does that mean?"

"That's who she protects," I said. "Would she like it if you set an intention to help the baby?"

"She wants me to. She's showing me how exhausted she is."

After setting the intention to help the baby who was protected by the overwhelmed part, I wanted Vera to have the opportunity to practice a different way of getting her need met before we stopped, so I returned to redoing her interaction with Peter. But first I asked him, "Does any of this make sense to you?"

"It does." He looked at Vera lovingly.

"Are you available for her to ask for what she needs from you?"

"I am," he said.

I turned to Vera, "Now that you're aware of what happens inside when you get home from work, would you try asking Peter for what you need by speaking for your overwhelmed part rather than from your angry protector?"

Vera nodded.

"Good let's try it again. Peter, in your very exuberant way, let Vera know that you and the kids really need her, right now, even before she puts her stuff down!"

After Peter did so, Vera took a deep breath, closed her eyes as if negotiating inside, and then said, "Okay. Peter, I'm really exhausted and a bit overwhelmed. I would love to take a shower, change my clothes and have a few minutes to regroup before I hang out with you guys. Twenty minutes maybe?"

"Sure," he said. "All you have to do is let me know what's going on and ask! But I have a request, too. I'd like both of us to talk to the kids in advance about doing this. I want you to tell them, too, that you just need to get out of work mode before you can be with us."

I looked at Vera, who bit her lip. "I know that's the right thing to do and it's totally reasonable. Why does it scare me?"

"Is this the part who has a hard time letting you ask for things?" I said. **"What do you say to it?"**

After a moment, Vera said "The kids will be fine with this. They just need to know what the deal is. And if they're not fine with it, we'll find out what the problem is and work it out together. We'll be the parents. Every person in a family has needs. We have to model that for our kids."

Peter, who looked a little surprised, said, "Yeah! I agree."

Over time, with sessions of practicing unblending and experimenting with new behavior, Vera cultivated the ability to make requests and say no, to tolerate signs of disappointment in Peter or the kids, and to recognize their bids for connection as invitations to be intimate rather than demands she needed to dodge. Peter, in turn, found that his sad, panicked response to Vera's *no* was a trailhead that led him to his own exile, a part who felt shamed for wanting to be seen and be close. Once he took care of this exile, his protector who tried to criticize Vera into compliance took early retirement and he became both more tolerant of her need to say no sometimes and direct about making his own requests.

Making a clear, direct request to have a need met can be challenging if that need conflicts with a need that is being expressed by the partner. Some people bully and make demands, others only hint at what they want, but neither method gets a positive result. In IFIO we teach partners to notice their needs either for connection or individual time and space, and to explore the childhood dilemmas that make it difficult to ask or say no in the present.

Noticing needs for connection means getting into relationship with parts and becoming their primary source of inner-connectedness (Schwartz, 2008). We teach people how to do this and how to make requests of the partner. If the other person is not readily available to meet the request, the vulnerable part is still securely connected inside. In my experience, when couples practice unblending and speaking with clarity, knowing that they can tolerate a yes or no in response to a request, their negotiating skills improve dramatically, as does the chance that requests will meet with an open hearted response.

How To

We all want to be understood and cared for by our partners, but couples often have needs that conflict and they become polarized when they are trying to get their needs met. When a couple presents with this dilemma, our first intervention is to normalize the situation and let the couple know that even though their needs conflict at times, they can learn a more effective way to negotiate getting their needs met. Essentially, we help the couple recognize that their needs are valid and that childhood experience is inhibiting them from asking and saying *no* more skillfully. Finally, we teach them to make inviting requests. Most couples need to practice these steps many times in your office before they can succeed on their own at home.

Teaching the Couple to Negotiate Needs

Step 1: Flesh out more effective ways of asking.

- For example, instead of, *I need more time with you,* try, *I miss you, I'd love to spend some quality time with you.*

Step 2: Track their cycle.
Step 3: Help reactive protectors unblend.
Step 4: Offer an invitation.

- For example, *If there was a way to negotiate needs between the two of you with less fear of either being trampled or abandoned, would you be up for learning how?*

Step 5: Begin by attending to one side of the polarization. Work with one person's protector while the other acts as a witness. Switch if necessary.
Step 6: Facilitate a conversation in which the couple unblends from protectors and practices negotiating a different set of needs.

Summary

When a couple is not well differentiated it is particularly challenging for them to listen to each other carefully. When they try to negotiate differing needs from an undifferentiated place, they are more likely to fall into childhood patterns of fight or freeze and more likely to try to negotiate by making a demand rather than a request. So we focus on helping them to differentiate. Success with differentiation sees the partners recognizing that everyone has the core need to be heard, seen and understood, and that their negotiating has been painful because, having been shamed for having needs in childhood and having parts who gave up on having needs met, they experience the partner's unavailability as a shaming rejection of their need.

As the partners feel more Self-energy and learn to meet some of their own needs internally, they gain room for error and forgiveness in the relationship. In turn, this helps relax the polarity between protectors who suppress needs and protectors who try to get needs met with demands. Once protectors relax, the couple is far more likely to make requests from the heart and tolerate limits, knowing that saying no (or yes) is not a survival threat, and that they can safely participate in the give and take of negotiating whose needs will take precedence at any given time.

9

SHAMING AND FEELING SHAMED IN COUPLE THERAPY

In this chapter we look at shaming and feeling shamed, which are inevitable in couple therapy and have a profoundly negative effect on intimacy. To create safety, the therapist must be fearless and able to stay present with vicious cycles of blaming and shaming. In IFIO, we pay close attention to protectors whose bastion against shame is shaming inside (other parts) or outside (the partner), and we work to unburden them as well as the parts they have savaged. When these parts do finally unblend, the couple has more room for self-knowledge and self-compassion and they can begin to see each other as a resource rather than a threat.

The Pain of Shame

We humans have a conundrum – we're hard pressed to survive without positive emotional connection (Siegel, 2003), yet relationships can be dangerous because we're so vulnerable to feeling shamed and, once shamed, our protectors often conclude that survival requires withdrawal. If so, they will exile parts with relational needs. Once a part feels that its needs are repellant and unacceptable, its misery and longing, coupled with its inability to disappear, just encourages protectors to double down on disconnection. The pain of shame can thus have a profoundly negative impact on relationships. In addition, once shame has been internalized as an accurate self-assessment, shaming protectors don't need an interpersonal interaction to induce the feeling, they recreate it themselves.

Shame Protectors in Relationship

Shame protectors, who focus inward and outward simultan-eously, are shapeshifters who are capable of taking on varied, numerous roles to try to prevent or distract from shame. Their goal is *never again* and they are often very evident early in couple therapy. They can be unyielding, intense and punishing, or passive and avoidant. But whichever strategy they use, their behavior can't get the job done. For example, rage, a frequent protection for shamed exiles, is profoundly alienating to others and papers over the self-criticism and self-loathing that is going on inside (Kaufman, 1980). Male clients often tell me that they feel safer denying shame than admitting that they are vulnera-ble to being shamed, which looks weak and therefore feels more shameful. In response to their rage, others tend to respond with denial, submission and withdrawal, or shaming in return, or some combination. Our goal is to help couples understand that their shaming and blaming cycles are actually misguided attempts to prevent the feeling of shame.

Working with Shame: The Therapist's Role

Being vulnerable, the hallmark of progress in therapy, is a great risk for couples because the partner is a potentially hostile wit-ness and the therapist is relatively unknown. Sometimes both partners walk in the door with the belief that vulnerability is weakness and their protectors are likely to be moved to punish any admission of sensitivity or insecurity (Sweezy, 2013). There-fore, in my experience, the therapist who is knowledgeable about yet unafraid of shaming and shamed parts will fare best. Although shaming is painful to witness and liable to evoke our own shamed exiles or shaming protectors, it's a big therapeutic opportunity – our ability to stay attuned to shaming and feeling shamed can make all the difference to therapeutic progress (Lewis, 1987).

THERAPIST TIP

Ask yourself these questions:

- What do I feel when I think about naming shame in a session?
- Am I comfortable acknowledging shame as it arises in my clients? If not, why not?
- What are my beliefs about shame? Theirs and mine.

The Effect of Shame on an Intimate Relationship

Shame has a far-reaching effect on intimate relationships. When the dynamic between shaming protectors and shamed exiles prevails, no area of a couple's life is left untouched. One partner experiences the other as a shaming caretaker from early in life and misses that the feeling is now being generated internally. Communication goes by the wayside, sexual activity suffers, and repair and forgiveness feel impossible – to name a few major areas of impact.

Healing Shame

Conscious awareness of – and differentiation from – the disowned parts who carry the burden of shame in the internal system is critical (Kaufman, 1980). Clients must get into relationship with their disowned, shamed parts. Internal security, which in IFS is called attachment with the Self, is key to restoring peace and inner harmony. Once parts form strong attachments to the Self, they stop fighting with each other. However, for parts to get into relationship with the Self we must heal not only relational injury but also the effects of inner perpetration by protective parts.

The final step in helping clients heal from shame is, therefore, attending to the protectors who have hurt other parts in the internal system as well as those who have hurt other people in the person's external relational system. They, too, have stories to tell and burdens to release. Only then, in my opinion, can we end vicious inner and outer wars.

Interrupting the Cycle of Shame and Blame

The following case illustrates some challenges I had when I was working with a highly reactive, shame-prone couple. I needed tremendous patience to help this couple unblend from the protectors who kept them from being able to acknowledge their needs for safety and connection. Throughout this vignette I illustrate interventions geared to help the couple regulate their fight-or-flight responses and interrupt their shame-and-blame cycle. I also point out some nuances in the use of the IFIO approach and discuss my internal process with some of my own highly charged protectors.

Working with the High Heat Couple: Alex and David

"He's just an angry man, that's all there is to it," Alex said, looking at me, "and I'm done with it. I can't take it anymore!"

During the momentary pause that followed, I checked with my parts. I knew from previous sessions that this provocation would evoke an angry response from David and I wanted to see how my anger phobic parts were doing. They reminded me that I should set the safety parameters, which I always do at the outset of a therapy, and which couples with highly reactive parts may need to hear repeatedly.

"Some reminders," I said. **"We have an agreement that you will both speak *for* instead of *from* your parts. Also you will wait until the other finishes speaking before you begin."**

"I can follow the rules," David said sarcastically. "I was in the military, remember?"

"I'm the one who interrupts!" Alex snapped. "You know why? Because you don't tell the truth – or at least you don't tell the whole story."

"Oh screw you," David said.

Alex rolled his eyes, "He's just an angry, sarcastic man."

At this point I noticed my stomach muscles had tightened

and a voice in my head was giving advice, "*This couple is out of control, do something quickly or they'll escalate!*" This part surfaces when I hear anger laced with sarcasm. I knew from experience that I would lose my Self-led perspective if my parts took over, so I needed to start by helping them to unblend. I observed my body and breath first because these bring me back to myself, the vantage from which I can trust the process and feel curious again. Next I sent a message to my parts, *I'm fine, I know how to do this.* And, as I felt the physical release that often goes with putting the brakes on my autonomic nervous system and unblending, I was able to turn my attention back to Alex and David.

At this point I was mindful that I would be interrupting them frequently until some measure of equanimity could be established and I wanted to assess if a modicum of unblending would be possible for them. I also wanted to get some context for their current anger. I started kindly but firmly: "Guys, I'm guessing something happened at home that has left you angry, upset and hurt. Am I right?"

"Yes and unjustly accused," said David.

"Will you tell me about it?" I asked.

"Yes," they both said.

"Who would like to go first?"

"Me," said David.

To prevent interruptions we must help protectors unblend, therefore I assured Alex's part (through direct access) that he would have an equal opportunity to speak. **"If David goes first, you will have a chance to respond and give your perspective, too."**

"Okay," Alex said. "I'm going to try hard to keep quiet."

"I was totally betrayed by him this week," David said. "I run the road association in our neighborhood. We have a lot of rules and regulations about how things are supposed to be handled. So I lost my temper and was asked to give up my position by some of the people on the committee and Alex sided with them. Totally! And now I'm out. Just like that."

Alex leaned forward and opened his mouth.

"Alex," I caught him, **"hard as this is, I'm going to ask you to hold on for just another minute or two."**

Alex leaned back, folded his arms across his chest and said "You're getting a distorted tale."

Noticing David's body language and wanting to bring his attention and curiosity to his somatic and emotional experience, I asked him, **"What's happening with you right now?"**

"I'm furious!"

"What do you notice in your body?" I said, seeing David's legs shake.

"I'm shaking."

"And what are you feeling?" I asked.

"This is not about feelings. It's about the truth!"

"So, **I hear you**. This is your truth about what happened, you have some energy going in your legs right now and you're furious."

"Funny you should notice," David said, looking away.

Although I felt drawn to stay with David I also knew that this couple could not achieve any equanimity without equal shares of my attention: *All parts welcome, no part more important than any other.* So I turned to Alex, inviting his perspective.

"Let me fill in one small detail," Alex said. "David leveled one of our neighbors during a meeting – which, by the way, he has done before – and that was it for them. They asked him to step down, which seems–"

"That man never does what he's supposed to do!" David exclaimed.

Part of my role is to help the couple maintain boundaries and uphold the contract that both partners get to speak and be heard, which meant that at this juncture I needed to ask David to wait. I was curious to see if he could.

"David," I said looking him in the eye, **"I'm going to ask you to hold on while I listen to Alex. I want to hear you both and I want to help you talk about this. But first Alex needs to be allowed to speak, too."**

"It was completely humiliating for me," Alex said. "This has happened before and I have always defended you."

Alex's ability to speak about feeling humiliated was an important warning sign for me. As shamed parts surface, the distress of protectors in both partners will increase, making them more likely to hijack a session. I knew that inside each of these men right now critics were ramped up and exiles were cringing.

"Okay," I said, "**I hear you**. This was painful and humiliating. I'm going to slow you down and ask the same question I asked David. **What is happening in you right now?**"

"*I'm* furious," Alex said through clenched teeth.

Since Alex had taken the risk of naming his feeling of humiliation, my job was to validate his courage and support his acknowledgment of a topic that we all go around the block to avoid. I generally do this with an *of course* attitude, using the word shame and its antonyms and generally treating the topic of shame as a subject worthy of interest and curiosity.

However, at this moment I heard a frightened part inside me say, *They're both really angry. It's getting complicated.* So once again I turned my attention inside. This time my part was afraid of failing the couple, which would of course evoke my shame. I let it know that I understood its concern but that these men didn't need to be *made to calm down* or be *managed* they needed to be heard, understood and helped to make sense of their pain. *Trust me*, I said to my frightened part silently.

As Alex and David struggled, their protectors were taking stronger and stronger oppositional stands. Because unsuccessful negotiations cause protective parts to become ever more entrenched in fear and anger, I wanted to hear how they had tried to process this event at home so I could flesh out their sequence and their hopelessness.

Leaning back in my chair, I said, "I hear that you're both angry about what happened. **What was it like to try to talk about it at home?**"

"Alex didn't get it," David said. "I was trying to do something important. The guy was screwing up and I was going to be responsible for his lapse in the end! What the hell am I supposed to do?"

"Is this how you try to talk about it?"

"Pretty much," David said.

"And what's it like to have it go this way?"

"Well, honestly, it's kind of this way all the time."

"Say more."

"What else can I say? It's just what you always see here," David replied flatly.

"What I see here doesn't feel good to either of you," I said.

"This is how we are," David repeated.

Turning to Alex, I asked, **"When you talked about this at home, what was it like for you?"**

"It was like talking to a red hot stone wall. And that's what it's been like for years," Alex said.

As I could clearly see, their pattern involved angry, judgmental parts barraging each other to cover for more vulnerable parts. Although this strategy provides temporary relief along with a feeling of power and control, hurt parts get reinjured and toxic polarities get reinforced. At this point, my main objective was to get them to notice the vulnerability under their anger.

"And **how do you feel** when you experience David as a red hot stone wall?"

"He's been angry with me … with the entire neighborhood for ages. It's like living in a war zone," Alex glared at David.

"Stay with me for a second, Alex. **I hear** you're really angry and that this fight, which has been going on for a long time between you two, causes you to feel like you're living in a war zone. **Are you with me? If you weren't angry right now, what might you feel?"**

"My chest feels tight and I have a knot in my stomach all the time. Sometimes I wonder if I'll have a heart attack. It just makes me ill. I can't even defend him anymore. It has to stop."

"What has to stop?" I asked.

"The raging," Alex said.

Since his protector was having a hard time giving any quarter, I decided to name their underlying vulnerability myself to see if they could acknowledge it, which might help their angry parts to step back.

"Okay let me ask a question. Is it true that you can both hear parts saying, *You hurt me and you need to change?***"**

They were silent for a moment and then both nodded.

"And you, David, have a part who is trying to get Alex to listen to you by yelling at him?"

"How else can I get him to understand?"

"Okay," I said. **"We hear that part."**

"And," Alex interjected, "I want him to understand why I can't defend him anymore."

"Okay," I said, **"this is another clarification for me. Both of you want the other to understand your perspective, right?"**

They nodded.

Turning to a question that evokes the fears and hopes of protectors, I asked, **"If your partner could** *get you* **then what? How about you, David, what would you feel if Alex really** *got* **you?"**

"I would feel safer."

"Safer?"

"Well, now I kind of regret saying that," David said. "I don't know what I meant." He looked confused, "What was your question?"

When a client loses his train of thought, rather than bringing him up to date immediately we may want to help him explore the moment. Getting lost can point to a part who has strong feelings, such as fear or shame, having surfaced along with a major protector, like dissociation.

"What just happened?" I asked.

"I got confused," David said.

"Is it okay to notice the confusion for a moment?"

He nodded.

"Check in with it."

"I sounded like a baby," he said.

"Wanting safety sounded baby-ish?"

"Weak," David replied, squinting at the floor.

"Actually, in my book talking about needs like safety takes courage," I said. **"When a wish makes us feel vulnerable it's not easy to speak of it."**

"Alex understanding me always makes me feel better," David said slowly.

"That makes sense," I said. Turning to Alex, I made a similar invitation so that we could hear the fears and hopes of his protectors. **"What is your angry part worried would happen if it didn't get angry?"**

"This behavior will continue and I'll feel isolated, not only in my marriage but in my community. All of our friends are just shocked. But," he added, looking at David, "I haven't heard you say anything like that for at least fifteen years."

"David likes feeling connected to you. What do you notice when I say that?" I asked Alex.

When vulnerability begins to surface, we hope it will invite the other person in, as it did Alex. "I'm sad," Alex replied. "What's happened to our relationship? It used to be so great. For the first five years we had a wonderful time. But it hasn't been that way since."

"You have a part who misses the wonderful connection you had with David early in the relationship."

However, it can also trigger more protection, as it did in David.

"He pulled back," David said with an aggrieved edge. Looking up now, he went on, "If he hadn't pulled back, we wouldn't be like this now. We were a team. Us falling apart is not my fault!"

"What are you feeling right now?" I asked him.

"He's blaming me."

Both partners had now named the experience of feeling shamed: Alex had felt humiliated by David's behavior with others, and David was feeling blamed (which is shaming) by Alex. In David's current state of mind, Alex softening had clearly made no difference. My goal now was to redirect their attention from the content of the fight to their habitual interactions and go back to negotiating with the fears of their protectors.

"**And when you feel blamed, what happens?**" I asked David.

"I tell him he's full of it."

"**And then what happens?**"

"He gets mad."

"-er" said Alex, "madd-er. I'm already mad."

"**And when your mad part gets madder, what happens?**" I asked.

"I restate the obvious *and* I make it clear that I'm fed up," said Alex.

"**What does your angry part think would happen if it didn't do that?**" I asked.

"He wouldn't hear me. Which he doesn't anyway."

"Do you know that part of Alex, David?" I asked.

"I do," he said.

"**And what happens to you when that part repeats something?**"

"I get furious."

"And you rage!" said Alex emphatically.

"True?" I asked.

"I guess," he said. "I feel like he's just trying to shut me up. He won't listen to me anymore."

When many parts are surfacing, unable to unblend and seeming to need more understanding and validation, I will suggest a pause to reflect on the big picture, make sure I'm hearing correctly and give those blended parts the message, *Someone is listening and understanding!*

"**I'm going to reflect back what I'm hearing and I want you to tell me if I'm getting it right**. David, I hear you have a part who feels devastated and betrayed because it seems that Alex is no longer standing with you or even listening to you. And Alex, I hear that you have a part who believes David isn't listening to you, although it thinks what you're saying should be obvious. So this part repeats itself and then feels shocked by his rageful response."

"That sums it up," Alex said.

David nodded.

Now it was time for me to reiterate that their fight was repetitive regardless of content and to invite them to try something new, with my help. **"And what just happened here today is similar to how you fight at home, right?** Neither of you feels heard or understood and, as a result, you both have an angry part who tries to force the other to listen. This escalates, is painful, and goes nowhere."

"Yes," they agreed.

"So it makes sense to me that you both want things to change," I said.

"Wanting is different from having," David said. "When I listen to you, I'm afraid I've turned into my father."

"Your dad was like this but you weren't – even though you were angry. I certainly didn't fall in love with your father," Alex said.

David put his head in his hands, "I don't know why I get so mad. Maybe if I didn't this would all be different."

"I can help you and your angry part. Are you interested?" I said.

"My father was a violent man," David went on. "I never wanted to be like him. But you know what? I actually can't imagine how to be any different now."

"That's okay," I said. **"I know how. Are you interested?"**

"Of course."

A man who has been traumatically criticized and physically attacked as a child will have entrenched protectors whose job is to ward off further shaming and injury. Those protectors need to be validated.

"When you get angry," I said, **"there's bound to be a reason. And I can help you to express what you feel differently, without denying anything.** This, in fact, would be a great gift to your relationships."

"My anger may seem bad sometimes but it has taken care of me," David said.

"I'll bet it has. Can you tell us how?"

"Getting away from my old man, coming out, not giving a crap what anyone thinks of me."

"Your angry part has protected you in crucial ways. We all need our angry parts when life is dangerous. But what if your angry part didn't have to do this alone now, if you could be there, too? Would it be interested to get to know you?"

"Okay."

"Where do you notice it right now?"

"In my arms"

"Ask who it protects."

David looked up, "Why do you say that?"

"Experience," I answered. **"How old were you when your angry part stepped up?"**

He looked back at the floor. "I was fifteen when I decided no one was ever going to get over on me again. I would not go on being terrorized by my father and treated like dogshit in school for being a fag. That's why I signed up as soon as I could. I wanted someone to teach me how to beat people up. I wanted to have muscles and I wanted to know how to use a gun. Preferably a machine gun."

He looked up slowly and met Alex's steady, now kind, gaze but lowered his head again, unable to maintain eye contact. "I guess I've always needed help. And this angry part was the only one who showed up ... until I met Alex," he said. "Even though I have no idea how – or even *if* it's possible – I want our relationship back. I love you and I need you. And maybe I do owe our neighbors an apology. The last thing I ever wanted was to be my father."

Noticing the shame that motivates a protector while refuting its damning judgment with kindness and compassion helps it to trust and unblend. Then we can track back to the exile and hear how it was shamed (Sweezy, 2013). With awareness comes unblending, choice and the freedom to live in the present and be different from the past (Kaufman, 1980).

Protectors tend to polarize around how to handle shame – some hide while others take the opposite tack by raging, blaming and accusing. But the true antidote to shame is self-compassion, which has the additional benefit of helping people take responsibility for their behavior and actions (Neff, 2011). We guide clients to invite injured parts out of isolation and into connection through compassionate internal witnessing. At the same time, we help shaming protectors feel safe enough to retire from the job. This all serves as an internal correction to the isolation imposed by shame (Bradshaw, 1988; Neff, 2011).

Helping our clients move toward self-compassion, however, involves helping them acknowledge and accept not only injured inner children but also parts who have defended against pain by continuing to injure other parts internally and by attacking other people externally. Ultimately learning to unblend from and forgive our protectors, no matter how grave the wrong they've done, opens the door to genuine self-love and the ability to take care of us (Kaufman, 1980). We cannot move beyond shame and self-hatred until we can practice self-forgiveness.

The therapy with Alex and David progressed slowly. I worked with them consistently for many months, practicing unblending from their angry protectors and frightened exiles. Little by little, their parts experienced their Self-energy and began to trust it, which improved their capacity to self-regulate when provoked. Because of David's severe childhood abuse and neglect and Alex's own traumatic adolescent experiences with homophobia, their journey in therapy was very challenging. But as they unburdened shame and practiced new behavior they were able to redevelop their connection and feel safe enough to care again.

How To

Being able to recognize shaming as well as compliance with being shamed in the moment, as it happens, is the most important skill. For this, the therapist must be able to help her own system unburden experiences of having been shamed (repeatedly, if necessary) and reorient or retire shaming protectors.

THERAPIST TIP

1. Listen for shaming, blaming protectors.
2. Make sure your contract is clear.
   a For example, *I am going to ask you not to interrupt, both of you will have a chance to express yourselves and tell your perspective.*
3. Notice therapist parts and help them to unblend quickly. Watch for your parts who feel overwhelmed or want to avoid the shaming or the shamed.
4. Begin unblending protectors by using *direct access* and focusing on the body. Validate both the role of protectors and the ways in which exiles have been wounded.
5. Reiterate their cycle (many times during a session and over time throughout treatment – see Chapter 3).
6. Validate their needs (see Chapters 7 and 8).
7. When you reach childhood predicaments, unburden shamed exiles and shaming protectors in the presence of the partner.

Summary

It takes patience, perseverance and an open heart to stay present when a couple's protectors are in battle mode. Their most intense parts will use shaming and blaming to protect against feeling shamed, with no sense of irony. Our job is to interrupt their attacks while staying mindful that vicious behavior is a protector's way of trying to keep vulnerable, shamed parts safe. We start with their external cycle, tracking their interactions moment-to-moment to help them unblend and ground, then we move to the U-turn so they can each get to know their protectors. Regardless of the pain these hard working parts have inflicted, they deserve to be understood and forgiven.

10

DEEPENING EXPERIENTIAL WORK

In this chapter we invite couple therapists to step even further away from the content of the couple's conflict in favor of intensifying their experience in the here and now. Experiential exercises help the couple deactivate the autonomic nervous systems, unblend, view themselves differently, and try on new behaviors with the help of the therapist.

Experiencing the Experience

As well as focusing on helping the couple understand their process and unburden their parts, IFIO creates relational experiences that support contact, connection and experiential learning. Our goal is twofold: we want each client to learn to unblend from reactive parts and we want them, as a couple, to practice new behaviors (with support from the therapist) and experience different outcomes. The willingness to try new behavior relies on protective parts unblending because inner differentiation leads not only to caring more effectively and kindly for one's own parts, but also to feeling more responsible toward others. When the couple achieves this willingness and proceeds to use new skills and have new experiences, the dynamic of their relationship will be changed both in the short and long term.

When the therapist remains focused on content, she may fail to notice emerging parts as they drift subtly (or not) into dysfunctional but familiar ways of relating. When we miss these moments, we miss some of our best opportunities to deepen experiential work. In IFIO, as in many kinds of couple therapy, we offer a variety of exercises that make use of therapy as a safe laboratory in which clients can experiment and learn. The practice and repetition of skillful, effective behavior in our offices and eventually at home creates a storehouse of success that will lead to lasting change over time (Lind-Kyle, 2009).

Although I was aware of Hakomi (Fisher, 2002), and Imago Relationship (Hendrix, 1988) therapies, both of which involve experiential exercises, it wasn't until I had used IFS with couples for several years that I began to notice some missed opportunities. At first I had a part who overrode this intuition. But as I was able to unblend from this inhibiting part and trust myself, I began to follow my intuition and ask my clients to try something new. I quickly realized that the success of this approach relied on my level of attunement. I had to be extremely sensitive and available to the internal experience of my clients. Since I could never predict exactly what was going to happen, I learned to work with my parts to unblend in advance so I could be open, curious and prepared to work directly with whatever surfaced. Necessary, too, was the permission of both partners throughout. Since one person can easily feel more confident or courageous than the other and these kinds of experiments can feel exposing and evoke shame, I learned to watch for compliant parts who had the urge to override fearful ones.

THERAPIST TIP

- Be aware of your own comfort level in experiential exercises. If you lead with parts who feel shy, awkward, inhibited or inflexible so will your clients.
- Work with your parts who feel hesitant or unsure before introducing an experiment to your clients.
- Check with your parts who want to push clients too fast, too soon.

Experiential exercises can be simple or complex. They evoke a range of strong feelings, including sadness, relief, fear, curiosity and even humor, that become trailheads for the deep inner work of both the individual and the couple. The feeling of success with an experiential exercise deepens both intrapersonal and interpersonal healing. Below is an example of an exercise I use to promote emotional contact.

Michelle and Juliet: Moving in Your Direction

These women had been together eighteen years and married for eight. They were peri-menopausal working moms with two teenagers still at home. Needless to say, life was hectic. Their presenting complaint was *We have no couple time anymore! We don't know how to prioritize each other.*

The first phase of their therapy focused on learning the principles of IFIO, unblending and speaking on behalf of overwhelmed, lonely, sad and frustrated parts. They agreed that having the time in therapy to slow down and communicate was priceless. But they also noticed that they avoided asking for or responding to needs for intimacy even in therapy sessions.

"Would you be available to try an experiment that focuses on understanding what holds you back?" I asked them.

"Can you say more?" Michelle asked, looking anxious.

"It sounds to me," I said, "like both of you have parts who long for more intimacy and parts who hold you back from being intimate. Even though you are now more aware than ever of your wish to feel and be closer, some part stops each of you from reaching out."

As they nodded, Juliet added, "I have to say it surprises me. I recognize it, but it also seems weird to me that we should be like this after all these years."

"Here's the invitation of this exercise: First you will practice unblending and soothing your protectors while allowing your partner to soothe you, too. Then you will tune in to your needs so you are aware of whether you want more or less contact. And, finally, you will ask for more or less contact without wounding the other person."

After they agreed, I went on, **"Take a moment first to do an inner scan. Notice any parts who might not be ready to give you permission for this."**

"I trust you," said Michelle. "But can we call a halt if it's too uncomfortable?"

"Absolutely!" I said. "The permission of your parts is everything."

This exercise involves three distinct steps:

1 Notice and track protective impulses.
2 Invite a drop to vulnerability.
3 Experience resonance, positive contact and notice the effect.

Step 1: Move Toward Your Partner and Notice Protective Impulses

"Okay you two," I said. "Let's start by standing up." Because my office at the time was spacious, I could move my chair back to make plenty of room for maneuvering. "Let's stretch for a minute and get comfortable. Then will you go to opposite sides of the room?"

They did so.

"Now in a minute I'm going to ask you to begin walking toward each other slowly. But here's the instruction: As you move pay **very close attention to your body and especially your nervous system.** Stop moving if you feel the impulse to move back or spring forward." I predicted to myself from experience that Michelle's parts would move quickly while Juliet's would be tentative. "As you begin walking toward each other, pay close attention to what you are paying close attention to," I added.

They laughed.

"It looks like we have our eye on each other, focusing on what the other person is doing," Juliet said.

"Great. Let's pause and understand that," I said. "Close your eyes and breathe to notice which of your parts is focusing on the other person."

Michelle spoke first. "I realize this is really common for me and I wonder about you, too, Juliet? I wait to see what she's going to do before I make a move."

Juliet nodded. "Though for me," she said, "it's waiting to see what you're *not* going to do and then I make a move."

"Ask your parts why they do that," I said.

"It's safer," Juliet noted.

"Okay good. Pay attention inside and listen to your parts.... What makes it safer?"

"If I can figure out what Michelle wants by watching her behavior, I can decide what I want to do that will control the outcome," Juliet offered.

"And how is that safer?" I asked.

"I know this sounds strange since I'm always backing up. But what I'm getting is that I have a part who monitors me so I won't want too much. It protects me from being disappointed when I'm rejected," she began to tear up.

"What's happening?" I asked.

"I'm so rarely in touch with that feeling of wanting more. I usually just know I'm afraid of having to give too much."

"Different parts," I said.

"Really different. One wants more, the other doesn't think any kind of wanting is safe."

Step 2: Encourage Vulnerability

"Would you be willing to say more about the tears?" I asked.

"I feel sad," Juliet said. "So much energy goes into this business of protecting me. I wish I could get those parts to relax."

"That's the journey. Thank you for being vulnerable." I turned to Michelle, "What's it like for you to hear Juliet?"

"It's a relief," Michelle said. "It always seems like I'm the one who's waiting and watching Juliet to see if she wants to connect. I can sense it, so I'm watching for the opening."

"Because?" I asked. "What is the story your parts have about all this?"

"Yeah," she said, "I could, well ... I mean I've been rejected many times for wanting too much."

"Does this make sense?" I asked, addressing them both. "Sounds like both of you have protectors who are being vigilant about the other person and watching carefully for rejection, not making a move."

They nodded.

"And," I said, **"do you know when your parts learned to protect you by scanning your environment?"**

"Early," Juliet said.

"Me too," said Michelle.

Both women had exiled parts who had received harsh messages about their needs for contact and connection at a young age. Juliet had coped by internalizing her needs and becoming overly independent. *You're better off alone,* said her parts. In contrast, Michelle's protectors adapted by learning to pursue relentlessly, *Any contact, no matter how uncomfortable, will do,* her parts said.

Understanding and appreciating protectors who show up during an experiential exercise helps them to soften. In response, hearts open and love becomes more available. Love, says Cozolino (2006), turns off the alarm system.

Step 3: Resonance

Juliet and Michelle had already moved closer and hugged for a moment. Smiling, they continued to hold hands as they turned toward me. When feeling safe, human beings have the capacity for *limbic resonance* – a complex, rapid, largely non-verbal exchange of information about our inner states and interpersonal attunement, which allows for a deep, personal connection, drawing emotions into harmony (Lewis, Amini & Lannon, 2000).

"What are you noticing now?"

"My body feels soft," said Michelle.

"Me too. Open. Less threatened," said Juliet.

"And?" I asked. **"What is your impulse now?"**

"To be close," said Michelle.

"Yeah," said Juliet.

"And does that feel different?" I asked.

"Very," Juliet said.

Michelle nodded.

"Good. **Breathe, notice and allow yourself to get the reference for this in your body,**" I instructed.

According to Porges's polyvagal theory (2007), the vagus nerve, or *smart vagus,* becomes activated under conditions of safety, allowing the body to relax. Even as we scan our surroundings for risks, a sweet smile with gentle eye contact and a soft voice with rhythmic inflections will cue the brain to regulate the vagus nerve. In response, the heart rate slows, breathing eases, stress responses switch off and people move closer (Porges, 2007). In IFIO language we would say that noticing and caring for protectors helps them to step out of the way so the nervous system can relax and the Self can become more available. In this state, partners have access to their inherent ability to give and receive love.

"Take time to practice so this becomes your new habit," I said.

With many more experiments like this in the office, and more and more at home, each woman gradually felt safer and more available inside and out.

Experiential Exercise #1

1. Explain the purpose of the exercise: *You wish to feel closer. We can practice that.*
2. Map out exactly what the exercise entails: *I am going to ask you to move toward each other and notice what happens inside.*
3. Create safety by getting permission from both partners.
4. Work with and help embodied protectors to unblend in the presence of the partner, and understand the part's impulses.

5. Encourage the expression of vulnerable parts: *Will you say more about your fear?*
6. As protectors soften, ask clients to notice what happens with less protection: *What are you noticing? What are you moved to do now? How is this different for you?*
7. Anchor the experience: *Allow yourself to breathe and notice what's happening in your body.*

THERAPIST TIP

- Pay attention to moments when your couple's process will be deepened by movement or a behavioral change.
- Always check for safety and get permission from both partners before engaging them in an experiment.
- Notice your confidence level: Can you stay present to whatever comes up during experiential exercises?

Damien and Justine: Redoing Conflict

Often when couples come to an appointment having been in conflict between sessions, they want to report what happened and who was to blame. The back and forth of *he said, she said* only gives protectors an opportunity to dig in further on blaming and shaming. To paraphrase their thinking: *If I can hurt you enough, you'll repent, feel what I felt, understand the error of your ways and love me like you once did.* Although these tactics activate the autonomic nervous system and leave couples with limited resources internally and together, their protectors adamantly resist the idea that such conversations do nothing to invite the other person's love.

Nevertheless, there are useful ways to help couples reconstruct and redo their conflict. The purpose is to help their protectors unblend so we can gain insight into the vulnerable parts they protect. As parts unblend, the couple has a chance to auto regulate or, as we say, be Self-led. From a Self-led perspective they can redo the conversation and listen to each other with curiosity and kindness. Here is an example of another experiential exercise.

"Whoa," I said after listening to Damien's protector raising his voice to get Justine's attention, "what's happening?"

"We're fighting!" Damien said.

"Would you like some help?" I asked, addressing them both.

"Oh sure!" Justine rolled her eyes.

"Okay let's do what we've done before: Slow it down, reconstruct and start over. Are you willing?"

"Yes," replied Damien.

"I said yes," Justine said.

"What's happening?" I asked.

"We have a dilemma. It needs to be addressed but Justine is sharp and unkind," said Damien.

"And you don't listen!" Justine exclaimed. "I have to communicate perfectly or you just freak out."

"What's the dilemma?" I asked.

"Basically," said Damien, "it's an ongoing thing. We have a ton going on right now and we constantly fight about who does what, when."

"Damien did his defensive thing and I blew," Justine added.

Human beings have two important survival skills that happen to interfere with relationships: we learn what is unsafe and we scan for threats (Porges, 2007). Once a learned threat cue is activated, the autonomic nervous system engages and we're no longer differentiating the present from the past, we're simply aroused (Cozolino, 2008). The good news is that human beings also have internal resources to calm the autonomic nervous system so we can engage from our center, in balance, with love and curiosity.

Porges's polyvagal theory proposes that human beings can learn to activate a branch of the autonomic nervous system called the ventral vagus nerve (the nerve of compassion). The ventral vagus calms the nervous system by providing brakes on the fight-or-flight response and the parasympathetic freeze state prompted by life threatening danger. All mammals are capable of limbic resonance and regulation as well as high alert. In other words, human beings (mammals that we are) can attune to each other's inner states and draw each other into emotional congruence (Lewis et al., 2000). In this model we use unblending to reach the spiritual resource of the Self, from which state the nervous system relaxes and couples can access love, which makes their hard conversations possible.

Since we had already worked on unblending, Justine and Damien were prepared for my instruction. And since we had been working together for many months and had a good bond, I knew I could push their protectors.

"First," I said, "I want to remind you of a few things. Both of you get to speak, and both of you will practice listening. But first and foremost, let's see if we can help those protectors relax a little and find some common ground. **Notice your body, take a breath or two, and reassure your protectors that they will be heard.**"

They both attended inward for a moment.

"Now," I said, "**I have an experiment for you. It's fine to decline but let me describe it first.** It has to do with letting your protectors blow off steam without hurting each other. It will require you to stand, move and get into your bodies."

"I like that!" said Justine.

"You're crazy, Toni. But I trust you, I'll do whatever you suggest," Damien said.

"Great. Please stand."

I put a strip of masking tape on the floor and asked them each to take a side.

"Here are the rules for your protectors. No words, no crossing the line and no touching. This gives your parts a chance to communicate through movement and sound. Still game?" I asked.

They agreed and each took a place on one side of the tape.

"Now embody those frustrated parts, the ones who are trying to help you get a need met."

They made eye contact and laughed, a first step toward activating the body's natural calming effect (Porges, 2007), or in our language helping aroused parts to unblend. Damien jumped in first, right up to the tapeline. He scrunched up his face and began flailing around, pointing at Justine. Justine responded by crouching and snarling silently before leaping up with her arms high in the air as if she had to make herself bigger. Then they were both jumping, pointing, sticking out their tongues, grunting gutturally and boxing the air until finally they broke out laughing and plopped down on the couch breathless. They sat close and Justine reached out to take Damien's hand. Then her chest heaved with a sob. Damien put his arm around her shoulder and she leaned into him.

"That's good," she said through tears. "I need to release that energy. Being mad at you is so exhausting." She curled into Damien's shoulder and sobbed more, then pulled her face out and said, "I just need a minute to cry."

Damien wrapped his arms around her and rocked gently. "I know I can be a bear but I don't intend to hurt you," he said.

Justine sat up, wiping her cheeks on her sleeve, "I saw a lot of meanness growing up. My father was critical of all of us and my mother was super critical of him. I guess judgment is my birth-right default."

"What is the relationship between your judging part and the part who is trying to get a need met?" I asked gently.

"It just wants Damien to do what I need," she said. Then, laughing at herself, she turned to Damien, "Isn't that fine? Why would you complain about something as simple as that?"

Damien smiled.

"Do you notice a relationship between a protector and a part who is trying to get a need met in you, too?" I asked him.

"No it's just her," he said, going deadpan. "I don't have needs."

Justine punched his arm gently and he ducked away in mock fear.

"Let's mark the issue of needs for next time. Seems that both the protectors we witnessed today are trying to get needs met for you two. And there are lots of ways to do that more effectively. But for today, would you like to redo the conversation you were trying to have earlier from this softer place?"

"Sounds good," Damien answered with a sigh.

Trusting that this couple was unblended sufficiently to have the conversation they needed to have and to negotiate what they needed without much input from me, I set it up and sat back. In turn, they spoke responsibly and listened well. The outcome of their conversation was less important, they reported at the end, than their mutual willingness to listen.

Experiential Exercise #2

1. Describe the experiment: *I am going to help you get in touch with and unblend from protectors so you can re-do your conflict.*
2. Help them notice protectors and encourage unblending: *Scan your body and breathe deeply. Reassure your parts and ask them to soften.*
3. Get permission, create safety: *I'd like to try something different. You are welcome to decline my offer.*
4. Describe the experience: *We'll invite protectors to embody and express themselves, without talking. You'll have an opportunity to speak for them later.*
5. Remain attuned and sensitive as parts with feelings emerge. You may want to slow the process down, help overwhelmed parts unblend or help the client(s) make sense of a feeling.
6. Remember that embodying parts often leads protectors to soften, which helps the client to gain perspective.
7. Encourage a different conversation: *Would you be willing to try having the conversation again?*

THERAPIST TIP

Sometimes experiments fall flat, lack impact on the couple or create more discord. If that occurs, ask yourself these questions.

1. Was the experience set up without first establishing safety?
2. Was safety really established?
3. Was the client's interest sufficiently engaged?
4. Were the protectors of one or both partners too reactive and too resistant to going inside? (Fisher, 2002)

Summary

The sessions described in this chapter cover just two of many possible experiential exercises an IFIO therapist might use. An experiential exercise can be quite simple, taking just minutes, or can be more complex, requiring an entire session. In either case, experiential work can be a great way for couples to get the feel of unblending, deactivating the nervous system and having Self-energy, from which perspective they have better insight and more willingness to take responsibility for their actions without being critical of themselves or each other. The move from *talking* about an experience to *having* an experience, which takes courage on the part of the couple and creativity and sensitivity on the part of the therapist, is worth the investment.

How To

1. Establish trust with the couple over time.
2. Challenge yourself to pay attention to places where the therapy might deepen with such an experiment.
3. Be creative, curious and confident in designing experiential exercises. Exercises might include, but are not

limited to, movement, drawing, touching (for example, touching two fingers), using the eyes to express the feeling of a part and then Self-energy, trying new behavior or language, or reconstructing and re-doing a conflict.

4. In any case, get permission from both partners to proceed and never push your agenda.

5. Describe your experiment and its purpose before asking your clients to participate.

6. Point out the ways in which protection is paired with vulnerability.

7. Look for moments of vulnerability and softening and slow down to deepen.

8. Depending on the couple's level of differentiation, you might want to review the skills of good speaking and listening from Chapter 4.

9. Help them to re-do their conflict once they are unblended enough to speak and listen with respect and curiosity.

These corrective experiences strengthen each partner's capacity to regulate their autonomic nervous system (Porges, 2007) and engage in limbic resonance (Lewis et al., 2000), which promotes feelings of safety, connectedness and intimacy.

11

WHAT MAKES A DIFFICULT
CASE DIFFICULT?

Because the process of judging something *difficult* is subjective, this chapter does not illustrate difficult case material but rather invites us all to ask, *What makes a case difficult?* We can answer this question by unblending and listening when and if our parts react to a couple's issues and dynamics in therapy. These issues may strike us as common or unusual, explosive or poignant. They include the couple's relationships with extended family members, parenting philosophies, money, sex, extramarital affairs, violence, separation, divorce, illness and more – all topics of potential significance to anyone, including any therapist.

Throughout this book we discuss strategies for helping clients regulate physiological arousal. Since we are the same as our clients – our parts react according to our experience – we also focus on self-regulation. When our parts blend because they over- or under-empathize, judge the client, feel frightened, angry or repulsed they interfere with our ability to stay present and available. The content that evokes any of these reactions – whatever it is – qualifies as difficult. Difficulty is a matter for personal introspection and continual learning and the techniques outlined in Phase 2 of this book apply to all possible scenarios, easy or difficult for you.

Therapist Parts vs. Parts of the Therapist

IFIO trainer Pamela Geib invites trainees to explore the difference between two sets of parts who commonly activate with couples. The first set is *therapist parts*. These highly trained parts come to the model with expertise and often have strong beliefs about the therapist's role as well as what makes a relationship good. Although we want to respect, acknowledge and call on therapist parts, we also want them to differentiate and unblend so that we can stay in a collaborative process with our clients. When we blend, the opinions of our parts about what is healthy and normal preclude us from being open to the differing views of clients. Therefore, in this model we work with therapist parts to let go of being the expert in favor of exploring the couple's beliefs and goals for treatment.

Examples of *Therapist Parts*

- Highly competent in specific models of therapy.
- Wedded to certain ideas about what is healthy.
- Attached to being the expert.
- Unable to trust the couple's Self-energy.

The second set of parts that Geib explores with trainees is *parts of the therapist*. These are the parts (both exiles and protectors) from the therapist's childhood who get activated by the couple's parts, as discussed in Chapter 6 on countertransference.

Examples of *Parts of the Therapist*

- Fears conflict.
- Got triangulated by parents or early caregivers.
- Projects childhood caretaker(s) onto one or both partners.
- Feels shamed for feeling incompetent.
- Hopes to have needs met by the client.
- Feels easily overwhelmed by affect or lack of affect.

The goal of noticing your parts is to recognize how the couple's conflict mirrors your own issues in relationship.

The following exercises are designed to help couple therapists explore situations in which either *therapist parts* or *parts of the therapist* become activated and the therapist ends up feeling that the case itself, the dynamic of the couple or the material is too difficult to handle.

Inquiry #1: Who is Saying, *This Case is Too Difficult?*

Therapists who feel stuck, overwhelmed or frustrated can make a U-turn and listen to the part(s) who are judging either the therapist's work or couple's parts (Roadmap A, below). The first clue may come when you hear yourself saying *I don't know what to do.*

Roadmap A: Take Time to Listen

Step 1: Take time to listen carefully and allow your confused part to communicate until it feels heard and understood. Note whether it is a protector with a judgment or a vulnerable part with a fear.

Step 2: If the part seems young, listen to its fears and invite more history. You may need to return to this part later to understand and free it from burdens.

Step 3: If the part is a protector, listen to it very carefully. Ask it to be clear about why it feels the way it does. Parts have wisdom. When we unblend and listen (from the Self) to their non-extreme message, we generally gain insight both internally and in relation to the couple.

Step 4: Ask your parts what they need so they can trust you. This will help them stay unblended so you can access their wisdom as well as the wisdom of the Self.

For example: A blended part might behave in a controlling manner because it feels a need to slow a couple down, yet ironically the same intervention would have been very useful if executed with Self-energy.

Inquiry #2: Assessing a Negative Cycle between Client and Therapist

In Chapter 3 we describe how to assess conflict between partners by tracking their negative cycle and then having them notice the vulnerable feelings that drive their reactivity. In a parallel process, we ask the reader to note which of his parts gets activated in relation to the case material: What are your impulses? What would you say or do with this couple? What drives your reactivity?

"I just don't know what to do with this couple anymore," Jo said in a supervision session with me. "This guy, he just won't shut up! I've tried everything."

"Frustrated?" I asked.

"Very," she replied.

"Would you be open to exploring what's happening in your relationship with this guy and the couple?" I asked.

"Of course."

"Take a moment to bring them to your mind's eye. Then watch them engage in the dynamic that causes you to struggle."

She closed her eyes and was quiet for a few moments.

"What happens to you as you watch them?" I asked.

"My stomach clenches."

"What's your first impulse?"

"To yell at the man."

"And what do you do?" I asked.

"Oh!" she sighed. "I try to control him. I'm stern."

"And when you get controlling what response do you get from him?"

"Well his wife loves it."

"And him?"

"He tells me to back off."

"And then what happens in you?" I asked.

"I act cold and pretend to be open but actually I'm collapsing."

"Shall we check with those parts?" I asked.

In the work that followed, Jo convinced her reactive protector to talk about its role and who it protected. She had been bullied in school as a child and recognized what she called a *power over dynamic* between this couple. Her protector's answer was to try a similar tactic with the husband. When this didn't work, she felt numb and went silent in the room. As she worked with these parts to unblend, she began to see alternatives and make different choices with the husband. In turn, he discovered that his talkative, controlling part was also protecting a bullied young exile.

In IFIO our motto is *when you feel stuck, do a U-turn and look inside*. Our cycles with clients are invaluable guides to overcoming therapeutic roadblocks. Roadmap B (below) is designed to help you understand how your inner world relates to the dynamic or content of the couple. Have a pencil and paper nearby to write or draw what you learn about yourself.

Roadmap B

Step 1: Understand the Cycle
Imagine a difficult couple. Bring them into your mind's eye. Remember the content of their conversation or the relational dynamic that makes them seem difficult:

- What happens in your body?
- What do you hear yourself saying to yourself about the couple, about you and about your relationship with them?
- What do you say or do with them and what response do you get?
- How do your parts respond?

Notice the cycle between your parts and the couple.

- Can you take responsibility for your role in the cycle and bring compassion to your parts?

Experiment by beginning an inquiry with your parts from a centered place. Ask these questions and remain curious:

- *What's upsetting about this couple?*
- *How do I hope to be of service to them?*
- *What am I afraid would happen if I relaxed a bit right now?*
- *Which of my parts is caught in the cross-fire with this couple?*

Step 2: Unblend

Strategies for unblending prior to a session:

- Prepare yourself ahead of time by taking a few minutes prior to the session to remember which of your parts get activated by this couple's presenting dynamic.
- Become very aware of the pairing between your protector and the vulnerability (the exile) to which it reacts.

In session:

- Learn to regulate your autonomic nervous system
  - Bring awareness to your body.
  - Talk to your parts, they will listen.
  - Reassurance and loving kindness will have a positive effect.
  - Try asking: *What do you need in order to trust me?*
- Set the intention to work with any parts who cannot remain unblended directly after the session.

Step 3: When Appropriate, Speak for Your Parts

- *I am aware of a part who was getting in the way of me being present with you...*

Inquiry #3: What if I Can't Help Them?

What if you can't? There are times when no matter how willing your parts are to unblend or how earnestly you get consultation, you still can't impact a couple in the way you want. Unless you lose self-compassion and blame yourself or your clients, that's okay!

In my experience, therapist parts feel pressure to succeed no matter what. As a trainer of therapists I've spent countless hours in consultation listening to clinicians shame themselves for not having enough of an effect on a couple. We are quick to blame ourselves when the couple can't or won't change their dynamic. But technique alone, no matter how tried and true, is not the whole recipe for successful couple therapy. The couple's full participation is also an essential ingredient, and it's one that you cannot command. All you can do is invite. When the shaming critic deploys during an impasse, directing its wrath toward you or the couple, it wants to be helpful but its voice prevents honest inquiry about either you or the client(s).

Because staying present with a shaming part to prevent more shaming takes courage, it helps me to remember that these parts have stories, wounds and burdens from years of being loathed inside and out. IFS teaches us that protective parts who have become extreme will soften when they feel respected and acknowledged (Schwartz, 1995). But when blended, these shamers can be slippery and hard to access. They will only unblend when treated to genuine curiosity (Roadmap C, below). Learning to accept, respect and love our parts is the goal of therapy for us just as it is for our clients. In IFIO we also emphasize that shaming parts have strengths and gifts, which can only be accessed when they have been healed and are welcomed back into the system. We can never move beyond feeling that we've failed until we make peace with our vulnerabilities (Kaufman, 1980).

Road Map C: Working with an Inner Shamer

Step 1: Find it in or around your body and unblend to the best of your ability while remaining focused on the sensation in your body.

- What's happening in your body and what do you hear yourself saying?

Step 2: How do you feel toward your shaming part? Do not stop working on unblending until you can feel some curiosity, and, if possible, some kindness and compassion toward this part as well.

Step 3: Ask the part what it hopes or intends for you.

Step 4: Ponder the pairing between your shaming and shamed parts:

• Is the shamer protecting a vulnerable part?
• Can you see, feel or sense the relationship between these two?

Step 5: Work with the shamer. If you can stay unblended, ask the shamer these questions in order to understand it better:

• *How old were you when you got this job?*
• *Under what circumstances did you get this job?*
• *What was it like for you back then? Would you be willing to share your history?*
• *What is it like for you to speak with me now?*
• *If there was another way to feel secure and confident and you could retire, what would you rather do?*

Summary

Clients come to couple therapy struggling with all kinds of problems, including children, parenting, relationships with extended family, illness, money, sex, extramarital affairs and more. We respond to their concerns and feelings according to our history. If our parts, including our therapist parts, feel over- or underwhelmed, our job gets more difficult. Know yourself and you will understand why a given case is difficult for you.

One certainty is that we're all imperfect and we all find some couples challenging. When we feel stalled, shaming and shamed parts tend to obscure our many choices, which include speaking for our experience, referring the couple, acknowledging that not every couple is ready to do therapy or beginning again with a clear mind and heart. Owning mistakes and making repairs is, in any case, crucial role modeling. In addition, sometimes we need to change tactics, get more consultation or do more training. Whatever tack you choose, remember that you will surely make a difficult case more difficult if you allow your shaming critic to blend and blame you or pathologize your clients. Instead, attend to unblending and loving yourself through the difficult moments.

PHASE 3

ENDING

12

REPAIRING RELATIONSHIP
RUPTURE

In this chapter we discuss apology, repair and forgiveness in intimate relationships. All couples experience conflict around the feeling of betrayal at times. Some betrayals are the small, every day misdemeanors that come from misattunement. Others, like lying or having an affair, are big. Because many people do not apologize or forgive well, we explore beliefs about apology and what makes a repair feel authentic. Although we invite shamed and shaming parts home throughout IFIO, the couple is only ready to engage in repair when they can see each other as a resource rather than as *the one who wounds* or *the redeemer*. At that point, we can begin to talk about forgiveness and self-forgiveness, which will ultimately open the door for each partner to take responsibility for injurious behaviors, great and small.

Renewable Connections

Conflict is normal in intimate relationships, and useful when it leads to honest conversation about its cause, how each person experienced it, and how it can be resolved. In short, conflict is an opportunity for mutual growth and understanding. We are not advocating a need for perfect harmony in relationships, *but a rupture that goes unacknowledged and leaves anger unresolved will do damage*. Couples need the skill to renew a secure connection when conflict occurs. Here we explore obstacles to apology and how to facilitate authentic repair.

What Makes Apology Difficult?

For many people, including therapists, just mentioning apology or forgiveness can evoke an array of parts. Clients often have parts who associate apology and forgiveness with either accepting blame or being too vulnerable. They say things like: *Apologizing means that I'm wrong*, or *This will be used against me later*, or *If I take full responsibility, I'm letting him off the hook, nothing will change and I'll get hurt again*. And the therapists who come to my trainings often have parts who say things like, *Apology and forgiveness have a religious connotation*, or *People who have been abused should not be made to forgive*, or *There are people who do not deserve forgiveness*. Like all protectors, these parts have valid concerns. What I'm suggesting here is that we listen carefully to the meaning parts make of any given topic.

In IFIO, we invite partners and therapists to explore apology and forgiveness in a safe and respectful way, listening and giving voice to all parts. We work on the assumption that one person never generates all of the conflict in a relationship. Each has protective parts who do not want to be seen as being *in the wrong*, and each is likely to be responding to the belief that conceding a point – being wrong – means *something is wrong with me*. In addition, when neither partner had examples of good relationships in childhood, they will not have learned that apology and forgiveness can be accomplished without losing control, security and safety.

Repair is Crucial

Couples usually engage in therapy with the hope that ending their conflict will prevent any more feelings of injury. They may have tried to bypass negative feelings and recapture intimacy by moving on without repair, which left their protectors on guard and added the weight of current injury to the baggage already carried by their parts who were burdened and exiled in childhood. Or, in an equally avoidant scenario, they may have tried skipping repair by apologizing badly to get it over with, either blaming each other for being insensitive, trying to justify their own behavior or being dishonestly self-deprecating. These tactics come from parts who are trying to help. But since the effective approach to maintaining intimacy is to repair rupture, we challenge them compassionately.

How To

Because there are many ways to make a sincere and heartfelt repair, each couple and instance will look different. Nevertheless, I can offer seven steps for moving a couple through the process of repair, including helping them to speak and listen well, to empathize with the pain of the injured partner, and to take responsibility for actions that have caused harm. The seven steps are appropriate for all levels of rupture, from serious betrayals like affairs to everyday relational aches and pains. Moving through the steps may be quick or take a long time.

Because a repair process often evokes shame for both, many parts can need attention along the way. And because forgiveness and self-forgiveness is a process that occurs over time, the steps of repair described below are more circular than linear in practice. The following case illustrates work I did over a long period of time with a couple who were struggling after one had an affair.

Ben and Jill

"How was the week?" I began.

"Jill told me that she had an affair five years ago. She confessed and now I'm completely freaked out!" Ben threw his hands in the air. "I don't know what I'm supposed to feel or do."

Jill reached for Ben, "It was a bad time. Can we talk?"

Ben recoiled, "A bad time? Like the time as I'm having right now?" He jumped up and strode toward the door.

"Wait a minute!" I called while Jill burst into tears. But he walked out, slamming the door. I took a deep breath. *It's okay!* I said to my shaken parts. As my heart settled, I pondered whether to start with Jill, who was sobbing near me, or with Ben, who I could see outside leaning on the fence.

Step 1: Creating Safety for Both Partners

I turned to Jill, whose chest was heaving as she tried to recover her breath. Handing her the Kleenex, I stayed quiet and watched.

"I had to tell him," she said, "it was eating me up. We've been coming here and things have gotten so much better. I felt I owed it to him."

"Does his reaction make sense to you?" I asked.

"Of course," she responded.

"Bringing it up now takes courage. **Are you available, with my help, to hear what this is like for Ben, no matter how hard?"**

"I am," she said. "I have my own hurt, which was part of the reason I did it."

"I'm sure this has a history," I said. "Let me go talk to Ben."

As I walked toward Ben, I noticed his body language. He was leaning against my fence, hands in his pockets, looking down at the ground in a posture that radiated anger, hurt and humiliation. *But*, my observer part predicted, *anger first!*

"Want to come inside?" I asked.

"I'm pissed!" Ben exclaimed. "What could she possibly say to me at this point? Jeez! I think I just have to go."

"You can definitely go if that's what you need to do. **No one is going to hold you here.**" I waited through a moment of steady eye contact. "Really. **If, on the other hand, you want to stay I will help Jill listen to what this is like for you.** I will help you sort this out. **It's your choice.**"

Ben chose to return to the office. He sat opposite Jill, jaw clenched and hands clutched.

He said, "I don't know why I'm even sitting here. There's nothing to say. I just cannot believe this! Of all the things you could do to punish me!"

"Punish you?" said Jill, losing the look of concern. "I wasn't punishing you! I was taking care of myself. You were focused entirely on work and pornography! So I found someone who was actually interested in *me*."

"You've got to be kidding.... You equate work and porn with an affair?"

"Guys," I said. "Let's take a pause. A lot has happened here in the last fifteen minutes. I want to see what we can do to help both of you say what needs to be said without leveling each other."

Turning toward Jill, I said, "You just revealed that you had an affair five years ago." Turning toward Ben, I said, "I hear, understandably, that you are shocked and angry." Looking at Jill again, I went on, "And I also hear that you were hurt and angry when you chose to get involved with someone else."

Validating both in this way, I conveyed the message, *What you have to say and how you feel in the moment is important and we can make room for both of you to speak.* In order to do this, I had to ask my overwhelmed parts to drop back – not because affairs frighten me or because I feel judgmental but because I tend to feel overwhelmed when protectors heat up and engage quickly.

I went on, "I suggest that you take time now to speak and, with my help, listen to each other about what's happening in you right now. As hard as it may be, **I am going to help you speak for your parts without damping them down or pushing the feelings away. But if a part starts to blend and attack, I'll call a time out**. Okay? Who wants to start?"

"You better," Jill said to Ben.

Ben looked at me. "I need help. I don't know if I can talk without flipping out."

"Thank you, Ben! It's great that you can speak for that part. I will help you."

Step 2: Speaking and Listening

The therapist begins by helping the couple speak on behalf of parts and listen from the Self (as described in Chapter 4). When one partner is invited to speak either for the angry, vengeful parts who protect injured exiles, or for the exile itself, the other partner must be well supported. Listening to the impact of one's behavior can be a great challenge. Your job is to reassure the listener (the transgressor) that you are there to help and that you will slow things down if her parts get overwhelmed.

THERAPIST TIP

Safety is critical for both partners, so take your time and check in often.

When an individual feels deeply hurt or betrayed, unblending can be counterintuitive and many protective parts will try to convince the person that being blended is safer than being vulnerable. In addition, the partner who is blended to the point of hyper- or hypo-arousal with shamed parts and their protectors will not be a competent listener. Validation and staying present to both partners is key to the couple's sense of safety and to convincing protectors that the process will be worth the risk of unblending.

Nevertheless, protectors can misinterpret an invitation to unblend because they believe that the therapist intends to exile painful or controversial feelings. Since my intention is actually to make room for all parts so I can help a couple remain in their conversation, I state explicitly that speaking for parts is not a covert approach to tamping down strong negative feelings.

"So," I said to Ben, "start by remembering to breathe. Just do that for a moment; there's no rush ... great. Take your time. **Let your angry part know that you are here to speak for it and to listen to what it wants you to know.**"

"I'm furious!" Ben said, looking at Jill. "I have an impulse to hit you but of course I won't. I don't get why you're telling me this now. Are you trying to absolve yourself?" He shook his head, "How humiliating! Who else knows?"

"Do your feelings make sense to you?" I asked in the service of helping him unblend.

"I guess so," he said.

I turned to Jill, **"What's happening inside as you listen?"**

"I feel torn. On the one hand, I know what I did was wrong. On the other hand, I have so much anger and shame about what was going on back then that I want to defend myself."

"That makes sense to me," I said. **"Would it help your parts to know that revisiting and healing your past injuries is key to this process as well?"**

She nodded tentatively.

"Hold on!" Ben interrupted. "Are you letting her off the hook?"

"You mean that looking at her injury might encourage us to condone her behavior?" I asked.

"Yes! That's exactly what I mean," he said.

"That's an important question. **Let me say first of all that I am neither condoning nor condemning either of you. My intention for the time we have left today is to help you listen to each other and talk about your feelings.** We will go on from there to see what needs to happen next. **But in any case in my experience our process will eventually take us back to some history for you both."**

"Yeah well it was her choice" he turned from me to Jill, "It was your choice to deal with your misery by having an affair! You're not going to blame me."

"I'm aware of that," Jill said. "I hate myself for choosing to have an affair and I want to make it right if I can."

Ben sat back for the first time. "Hearing you hate yourself actually feels good. Right now I hate you too."

The session ended with mutual acknowledgment that they had a lot of sorting and talking to do. Ben asserted that he had no commitment to stay in the relationship, while Jill admitted that she was thoroughly ashamed and terrified that he would leave. Although I hope therapy sessions will end more neatly, with parts feeling safe and partners feeling connected, the opposite can certainly happen. Sometimes people leave my office feeling blended with hopeless, angry or vengeful parts.

Step 3: Self-Inquiry and Self-Forgiveness

Genuine repair requires the listening partner (the transgressor) to do a U-turn in order to discover what motivated his behavior. Therefore, once injured parts have been spoken for, we encourage the listening partner to understand and forgive his parts who transgressed before attempting an apology. Self-forgiveness, which is key to good repair, is not about condoning bad behavior. It does involve understanding why a protector felt the need to act, recognizing that its motivation was altruistic, and inviting it to choose a new role in the internal system. Apology is made more feasible for clients who understand that parts exist (a part is not the whole) and that they are motivated to help: *The part of me who behaved badly was misguided. I can help that part, and I am not bad.*

To achieve full forgiveness we must accept and love our parts who are capable of doing harm, especially our relentless critics who judge other parts and people. This can, of course, be a challenge for everyone in the room. The injured person often feels angry, while the transgressor feels defensive and ashamed. Meanwhile, the therapist may be in the grip of any number of strong feelings. Approaching hurtful, shaming parts can be dysregulating because they hold an especially corrosive and disgraced position in the internal system. In consequence, they need as much Self-to-part connection as any exile.

Over the next four sessions, Jill came alone. Ben moved to a friend's house and felt unsure about returning to therapy. I called to assure him that he was welcome back if and when he felt he could come. I also referred him to an individual therapist for support. Meanwhile, Jill and I continued with therapy, observing her polarizations and exploring the part who had chosen to deal with her feeling of deadness in the relationship with Ben by having an affair.

"I can't separate anger from shame," she said during one session. "As soon as I start feeling bad about what I did, I get mad.

I'm not sure who I hate more, me or Ben? It's like I need to find someone to blame."

"Shall we listen to that part?" I asked.

Going inside, Jill heard not only from the blaming part but also from parts who felt inadequate and useless. Feeling *less than* (or shamed) in her relationship with Ben, particularly when it came to sex, led her back to adolescent experiences of being ridiculed and humiliated by boys about her weight. It turned out that Jill had a long history of feeling ugly and stupid. And although she did not excuse the behavior of her shame protectors, she came to understand their impulse as an attempt to take care of an exile who felt worthless.

"How sad!" she said. "That fat girl wanted redemption. Maybe I *was* trying to punish Ben so I'd feel better about myself. I've used joyless sex in the past to prove I was worth something."

"How do you feel toward the sad girl and her protectors now?" I asked.

"Tender," she said.

Step 4: Authentic Apology

The most effective apology is a product of empathy and true remorse, which comes naturally if the other person's pain makes sense. Urgency, especially the urge to get it over with, is the enemy of apology. And confession is simply a different animal: "When you confess, you admit wrongdoing, when you apologize you express remorse" (Abrahms Spring, 2004, p. 152). The first step in the IFIO approach to apology is for the listener (the transgressor) to empathize and understand her impact. The therapist first garners everyone's Self-energy by unblending parts who are attached to ideas about right and wrong and will be judgmental, and then helps the listener (the transgressor) understand the effect she had on the vulnerable parts of the speaker (the injured person). This is much easier to do if the couple understands that the goal of apology is not to address self-worth but to acknowledge impact. If the listener (the transgressor) is protected from having her self-worth called into question, internally as well as externally, during this process she is far more likely to be able to take responsibility.

We also help the listener to consider and be curious about what the speaker (the injured person) might need to hear. Some people are fine with *I'm sorry*, while others prefer *Your feelings make sense to me given what I did (or said)*, or *I wish I had done it differently*, or *I will work on changing my behavior*. As long as the speaker feels understood and believes that the listener is genuinely sorry for having caused pain, the repair will have meaning.

THERAPIST TIP

- Watch out for your parts.
- Therapist parts who judge or shame one of the partners are blocking Self-energy and will evoke protectors.

When the listener (the transgressor) makes an effort but cannot take responsibility or achieve a genuine apology, it's time to explore how her protectors view apologies. Although the listener's inability to make a repair may be jarring and painful for the partner who feels injured, it's an opportunity to explore experiences and beliefs that relate to taking responsibility and initiating repair, without which no significant progress is possible in any case. Therefore, we reframe the stuckness of the listener as an important trailhead and an opportunity. This was not a problem for Jill, since she did listen to Ben and was able to deliver a sincere apology that included feelings of remorse.

"I'm available to listen to you," Jill said to Ben. "You haven't spoken to me since we left this office almost a month ago."

"I appreciate the invitation," I said to Jill, knowing that she was unlikely to get any thanks from Ben at this point. "Ben, are you ready to talk to Jill about the impact of her affair?"

I reminded them both about the ground rules for speaking for parts and listening from the Self (see Chapter 4) and assured them again that I was there to help them disarm as needed.

"What can I say? This was about the worst thing you could do to me," he said.

Having had a month of sessions with me, during which time she had heard from her parts about their sense of injury, Jill was now able to stay unblended and express true regret, apologizing to Ben with less of a confessional bent and more sincere remorse.

"I know I hurt you," she said. "And I know you'll still feel hurt and angry after I apologize. But I do want to make this right. I was chicken. I didn't tell you what I was feeling or give you a chance. I was also mad and I had an affair instead of speaking up. I want you to know that I feel terrible about treating you that way."

"I believe you're sincere," Ben said softly. "But I feel humiliated. I can't trust you."

"Tell me what you need from me to make this right," Jill said.

"Apology and forgiveness is not a one-time event," I intervened, anticipating that Ben was not yet ready to have that discussion. "I understand you have some parts who don't trust Jill. **I never push anyone to forgive before they're ready – if ever.** But perhaps trusting her isn't the top issue right now. Can I ask if you trust yourself?"

"What do you mean?"

"What do you hear yourself saying about you now?"

"How could I be such a fool?"

"You have a part who believes you were foolish and got hoodwinked?"

"Yes."

"Because you were blended with a too-trusting part?"

"Yes."

"Could we help these parts, Ben?"

He shook his head, "They're saying, *No.* This shouldn't be about me. She's the one who misbehaved."

"So you have more feelings and more requests to make of Jill?"

He nodded.

"I understand. But I also want to take time at some point, when your parts are ready, to help with what happens inside you."

Step 5: Setting an Intention

The next step is to help the listener (the transgressor) who is working on authentic apology set the intention to notice, understand and heal the part who caused the injury so that it will not repeat the behavior (Schwartz, 2008). In the process, we help the speaker (the injured party) shift his language from *blaming* to asking the listener to *take responsibility*. Because this approach is empowering for the speaker and de-shaming for the listener it opens the door for repair.

"Jill," I asked, "do you understand why you had the affair?"

"Yes, I do." She looked at Ben, "It was a misguided attempt to take care of some parts who were hurt a long time ago as well as in our relationship. I'm going to keep working on this because handling it that way didn't fix my problem and I never want to hurt you intentionally again."

Step 6: Forgiveness

Forgiveness requires compassion and understanding from both partners and, depending on the circumstance, may or may not be difficult. Begin this step by helping the speaker (the injured person) acknowledge parts who feel hurt, sad or afraid. These parts must not be ignored or sidestepped. At the same time, notice any parts of the speaker who are committed to feeling victimized and blaming the listener – these parts will need help to unblend.

In my experience, when the speaker (the injured person) refuses the listener's apology, he is likely to have some or all of the following misconceptions: that refusing to accept an apology will keep him safe from further injury; that forgiveness equals approval; or that forgiveness is a form of compliance. In contrast to this protective stance, we want both partners to understand that we can condemn a person's transgression yet forgive the person, and that forgiveness is not mutually exclusive with self-assertion, should the behavior occur again. The alternative of staying blended with protectors prevents repair and reconnection and is entirely counterproductive for the couple's goals in therapy.

In IFIO, the compassion of the Self allows us to accept, love and care for angry or fearful parts, and to care deeply for ourselves without losing connection with others. Most of us have at some time suffered violations that seem unpardonable. Refusing to forgive may feel to our protectors like an important show of strength, and it often provides a temporary rush of power. However, our protectors are mistaken. In reality, non-acceptance keeps the injured person tethered to the person who has transgressed, cementing the fixation of protectors on the danger of being wounded again by the partner (Abrahms Spring, 2004). It also ensures that the problem (the feelings of the exile) goes unresolved. Forgiving when we feel wounded is actually a courageous and wise act of self-compassion.

"I'm not ready to forgive you," Ben said, reiterating the message he had started with. "You don't deserve to be forgiven. I'm not letting you off the hook. Probably ever..."

Since we had now spent many sessions unpacking Ben's sense of injury while Jill answered his questions and took responsibility for her actions, I decided it was time to help Ben explore his beliefs about forgiveness.

"I hear you say you will never let Jill off the hook. Can you tell me what you mean?" I asked.

"She can never feel that what she did was okay," he answered.

"So," I said, **"if you forgave Jill you believe you would be saying what she did was okay?"** I asked.

"Absolutely," he replied.

"I'm not going to put any pressure on you to forgive Jill, that's entirely up to you. However, I am struck by your understanding of forgiveness. Where did you learn to think of it that way?" I asked.

Ben paused for a moment.

Jill interjected, "You might never forgive me. But I don't know what more I can do. If you can't trust me again or forgive me, I don't know if our relationship is sustainable."

"Who's speaking?" I asked her.

"I am," she said. "I want to mend this and make our relationship, which wasn't good before this happened, better. We have that opportunity."

"I'm afraid," Ben said.

"Thank you, Ben," I said. "Will you say more?"

"I do not want to have to go through this again."

"Go through what again?"

"I know it doesn't sound logical. But I have a part who's afraid she could have another affair," he said, looking at me rather than Jill.

"Okay. Can we listen to that part?"

"I think that's it. It wants to prevent another betrayal. It protects my heart."

"Protecting your heart is important," I said. **"Without asking it to go away, would it move back just a little, soften up a tiny bit for a few minutes?"**

He closed his eyes and took a breath, "I want to stay angry. It's more powerful than feeling humiliated."

"You have a part who feels humiliated," I said.

"I do," he said.

"What if we could help it?"

"Yes?" Ben said, opening his eyes.

"We have done some work with this part over the past months. Sounds like it still has a big fear of being hurt and shamed," I said.

"That seems to be true," he agreed.

"Okay," I said, "we're near the end today so let's set the intention to help the part who feels humiliated next week. We know some of its history and I suspect there's more." Then I went on, "My invitation to you both as you leave here today is **to stay connected to your hurt parts. Our goal is for them to**

trust that whatever happens out here, they are okay inside with you."

"That's nice but I can't imagine I wouldn't have a big reaction if Jill ever betrayed me again," he said.

"I'm not planning on having more affairs," Jill responded. "But I will surely hurt you sometimes. And you'll hurt me, too."

"If you do have another affair, I'll leave," Ben said.

"I would expect you to."

"Ben," I said, "can we ask your faithful protectors to soften a bit so you can hear what Jill is trying to say?"

Ben took a deep breath, then turned slightly toward Jill and said, "Okay."

"I want you to believe that I'm sorry and I regret hurting you," Jill said, with tears in her eyes. "I'm asking you to forgive me."

For the first time in this interaction, Ben looked at her. "I need time," he said, the anger gone from his voice. "But I know you mean it."

If the speaker (the injured person) is struggling or feels adamantly opposed to accepting the apology, you can ask if he is willing to take in just a small amount of the regret from the listener (the transgressor). In addition, if you remind the speaker that the listener is trying something scary and different with this apology, he may at least be willing to acknowledge that the apology is sincere. In any case, the speaker may need a lot of time to explore his feelings before being ready to accept or forgive. Forgiveness is a process that occurs over time and apologizing is a step in the right direction, though it won't necessarily bring forgiveness.

Step 7: Shared Responsibility

Conflict is never one-sided and neither is damage. The speaker (the injured person) will eventually also need to examine and acknowledge his role in any patterned conflict. This is a delicate step that often requires patience from both the listener (the transgressor) and the therapist. In my experience of watching couples handle betrayals of loyalty, the injured person is often devastated on so many levels that protectors are loathe to step aside and allow any sharing of responsibility, though he may feel more willing after the partner offers an authentic, heartfelt apology, and changes her behavior.

Our goal over time is for the couple to understand that relationships are a collaborative creation and that sharing responsibility provides a solid basis for beginning again. Ben and Jill continued working with me, witnessing each other's internal work as well as listening, speaking and exploring their relational needs more skillfully. They explored childhood issues related to betrayal, fear of abandonment and feeling shamed. And they became interested in how hurt and disconnection in their marriage had led to their extreme behaviors. Eventually, Ben admitted that work and pornography were an exit strategy for him, although he was hesitant to use the word *affair*. This courageous couple chose to stay together and use the fallout from Jill's affair to transform their relationship.

Summary

Conflict is normal in close relationships but many adults have had no role models who were capable of making an authentic apology. They do not know what it takes to repair a misunderstanding, let alone a deep betrayal. What makes repair difficult for both people, in my opinion, is the fear of more humiliation and pain. When a couple locates the Self-energy to tolerate this fear and goes forward with the process of apologizing, forgiving and sharing responsibility, they find it transformative even if it leads to a conscious parting of ways.

The seven steps outlined here can be used with serious betrayals or small ruptures. It can take moments, months or years to close the cycle of conflict and disconnection with heart-to-heart connection. In any case, forgiveness, starting with self-forgiveness, denotes the end point of a process that brings shamed and shaming parts the Self-to-part connection they crave, which in turn allows the individual to take full responsibility for his behavior.

Seven Steps to Authentic Repair

Step 1: Creating Safety for Both Partners

- Withhold judgment and send the message:
  - *I can help you and hold both of you and all your feelings* (anger, hurt, betrayal, fear, shame, et cetera).

Step 2: Speaking and Listening

- Help both partners to unblend so they can speak on behalf of parts and listen from the Self.
- Protect each partner from shaming and feeling shamed by setting up good habits of speaking and listening (Chapter 4):
  - *Can you speak authentically without causing harm? Are you able to listen without collapsing into shame or defensiveness?*

Step 3: Self-inquiry and Self-forgiveness

- Help the wounding partner to safely make a U-turn and begin exploring parts who caused harm.
- Send the message:
  - *A misguided part of you did this, and though its behavior was bad, you are not bad. We can get to know, understand and help this part.*
  - *It is possible to take full responsibility for your actions and also to forgive yourself fully.*

Step 4: Sincere Apology

- Help the listener understand the impact of her behavior, and access and express empathy and remorse.
- Apologies laced with shame will sound insincere and are more likely to be rejected.
- Help the person who is apologizing to continue working with self-forgiveness and healing shamed parts (Chapter 9).

- The listener (the transgressor) will have more access to empathy when he can tune into the hurtful impact of his behavior.
- Unblending from shame and defensive parts is key:
  - *What words does your partner need to hear to feel understood and to receive your apology?*

Step 5: Setting an Intention

- Help the listener (the transgressor) to assure her partner that there is a plan to work with the part and an intention to end habitual behavior:
  - *Are you interested in getting to know the part who does this?*

Step 6: Forgiveness

- No one should be pushed or pressured to forgive.
- Forgiveness is not letting someone off the hook; it is a choice to let go of anger and resentment.
- Forgiveness can be healing and requires compassion for oneself and the other.
- Forgiveness may have many meanings to an individual. For example,
  - *I will feel more empowered and protected if I keep my heart closed.*
- Help explore the parts with beliefs about forgiveness. Offer a possibility:
  - *To forgive is to live with an open heart; you are not condoning the behavior.*
- If someone believes he will never be able to forgive, this may be a useful point of exploration.
- If a person refuses to forgive, their partner may feel that she is perpetually begging for mercy. Encourage him to do a U-turn and empower himself.

Step 7: Shared Responsibility

- The idea that a couple shares responsibility in conflict may be challenging for the injured person. Take your time with this step. If the other steps in the process have been successful this one may evolve naturally.
- Extreme behavior may be rooted in history.

Our goal over time is for the couple to understand that they have created their relationship collaboratively and they can recreate it with a stronger foundation.

Conclusion

IFIO couple therapy relies on you unblending and filling with Self-energy so that you can hold your parts firmly and tenderly while supporting your clients' parts to unblend and experience something new: being separate and connected, different and acceptable, supportive and self-reliant, unique and together. Our blueprint specifies no single route or preset time frame, but we do suggest keeping certain tools handy as you go: tracking relational dynamics, inside and out; speaking for parts and listening from the Self; becoming comfortable with deep intrapersonal work as part of couple therapy, being aware of countertransference; and, for everyone in the room, unblending, unblending, unblending. To be present and self-accepting is to be available and open hearted, inside and out. From there, we can help couples do the same with themselves and each other.

APPENDIX 1
Unblending

We use the term blending in IFS and IFIO to describe how parts take over the conscious mind. In and of itself, blending is neither good nor bad, it is the natural relationship of the Self with parts. When we have difficulties in life, however, parts can develop extreme feelings or beliefs and take over internally, flooding the internal system, blocking the Self, obscuring clarity and overwhelming us emotionally. Shame, in particular, tends to evoke extreme protectors who blend reflexively and hold on tight. They require a lot of unblending practice.

To understand what we mean by blending and unblending, experience is the best guide: Feel, sense and observe the phenomenon in yourself. When you attend to and notice (that is, unblend from) your parts, your conscious awareness (your Self) may take on a spatial quality. The Self can be with parts in this space but also, like the tide, parts can move into this space and take it over, either gently or with force. When the tide recedes, the presence and spaciousness of the Self will return unless another part blends and takes over. Blending is not, in and of itself, a problem. To function deftly in response to our environment, we need our parts to have flexibility and flow, to offer their strengths and lean into the inner resource of the Self. But when extreme parts take over and block the Self, problems do tend to develop.

We know that once we've built the caring, non-judgmental Self-to-parts relationship that heals, our parts no longer fear unblending. The rub is that we have to convince wary protectors to try. We do this with patience, inviting them to differentiate (using words like *relax* or *separate*) so they can get the feel of being connected with the Self. Our goal is for burdened parts whose blending has become a problem to form a strong, permanent, healing attachment with the Self, unburden, and find welcome for their own special resources in the internal community.

APPENDIX 2
Unburdening

The word *unburdening* describes a process, often but not always framed by ritual, in which a part who feels securely attached to the Self lets go of painful, extreme beliefs and feelings that developed during difficult or traumatic experiences in the past. When successful, an unburdening makes room for true self-love and compassion (Schwartz, 1995).

Clinicians new to IFS can be challenged by the notion of dramatic shifts in feelings and behavior after a part lets go of its pathogenic beliefs, and they are concerned that undue optimism will mislead and disappoint the client. In our view any dramatic shift that occurs when a part unburdens is the result of an incremental process of change that has been occurring throughout the therapy. Just as a wedding celebrates the new status quo after courtship, the ritual of unburdening marks a new status quo after the Self has succeeded in wooing protectors and joining with exiles. Of course, not all parts stand on ceremony; some unburden right away when they experience the Self-to-Self connection. When this happens in couple therapy we call it a *relational unburdening*.

In either case, with or without ritual, the capacity to let go of disproved beliefs and outdated emotional reactivity is a developmental milestone, which we want to tag in the memories of our clients and reinforce in any way we can.

GLOSSARY

Although parts are considered autonomous and their behaviors motivated, there is no empirical view in IFS on the nature or origins of psychic multiplicity, nor is there any consensus among practitioners about what a part is. Therefore, the IFS portrait of independently motivated parts at this point remains an invitation from Richard Schwartz and other practitioners of IFS to risk acting as if the matter is settled because doing so is clinically effective.

SELF: The innate presence in each of us that brings balance, healing and compassion and other nonjudgmental, transformative qualities (the 8 Cs below) to the inner system. While parts can blend with (overwhelm and obscure) the Self, the Self nevertheless continues to exist and is accessible as soon as parts unblend.

Qualities of Self: The 8 Cs

1. Curiosity
2. Caring
3. Creativity
4. Courage
5. Calmness
6. Connectedness
7. Clarity
8. Compassion

SELF-LEADERSHIP: Self-leadership is occurring when an individual has the capacity to hear, understand, be present and be in relationship with all parts, acknowledging and appreciating the importance of their roles in the internal system and in relationships with other people.

PARTS: Internal entities, or subpersonalities, who function independently and have a full range of feelings, thoughts, beliefs and sensations. These entities, who have their own Self-energy when they feel understood and appreciated, vary in appearance, age, gender, talent and interest. They exist and take on various roles within the internal system. When not exiled, or in conflict with each other due to protective intentions toward exiled parts, they contribute in a variety of ways to our efficient functioning and general well-being.

THREE TYPES OF PARTS: IFS classifies parts in three broad categories according to how they function in relation to each other. An injured part, or *exile*, is both vulnerable and primary in its influence on the behavior of other parts. Orbiting around exiles are two categories of protective parts. The proactive protector, called a *manager*, has the role of maintaining the individual's functioning despite what the exiles feel. The reactive protector, called a *firefighter*, has the role of suppressing the emotional pain of exiled parts when it breaks through despite the best efforts of the manager.

VULNERABLE PARTS: 1 *Exiles:* Revealed in feelings, beliefs, sensations and actions, these parts have been shamed, dismissed, abused or neglected in childhood and are subsequently banished by protectors for their own safety and to keep them from overwhelming the internal system with emotional pain. A great deal of internal energy is expended to keep exiles out of awareness.

PROTECTIVE PARTS: 2 *Managers:* Proactive helpers who focus on learning, functioning, being prepared and being stable, and are therefore vigilant in trying to prevent exiles from flooding the internal system with emotion. As a consequence, they often use a variety of harsh tactics – not least, relentless criticizing and shaming – to keep us task-oriented and impervious to feelings.

3 *Firefighters*: Reactive protectors who share the goal of exiling vulnerable, injured parts and extinguishing their emotional pain. Firefighters get activated when the memories and emotions of exiles break through despite the repressive efforts of managers. They tend to be fierce and use extreme measures that managers abhor, like alcohol and drug abuse, binge eating, excessive shopping, promiscuity, cutting, suicide and even homicide.

BLENDED: When a part is undifferentiated from the Self.

UNBLENDED: The state of being in which no part (that is, feeling, thought, sensation or belief) is overwhelming the Self. When unblended parts remain present and accessible but are not vying to be dominant, we have access to the qualities of the self. The state of being unblended is often experienced as internal spaciousness.

TARGET PART: The part the client chooses when beginning an exploration. We help the client remain in contact with this part unless other parts make it too difficult. When this happens we contract to change the target part and the objective for the session changes, but we remain aware of the original target part and return as soon as possible (which may be another session).

POLARIZATION: An adversarial relationship between two parts who are in conflict over how to get needs met. Over time, their opposing views tend to become increasingly extreme and therefore costly. However, when the client's Self acknowledges the positive intentions and contributions of each part, they will generally be willing to allow more Self-leadership. Internal polarizations are manifested between the couple as well as inside both partners.

DIRECT ACCESS: When parts are unable or unwilling to unblend, the therapist speaks directly to the client's parts. In direct access the therapist can speak *explicitly* to a part (for example, *Can I talk to that part directly?*) Or, when the client rejects the idea of parts, or says, *That's not a part, that's me,* the therapist can speak to it *implicitly*, without acknowledging it as a part.

BURDENED: When parts have accepted painful beliefs and feelings about themselves from external sources and feel no relief until they are unburdened.

WITNESSING: The process of a part showing and/or telling the client's Self about its experiences until it feels understood, accepted and self-accepting.

UNBURDENING: The ceremonial process by which the painful emotions and harsh self-judgments of an exiled part are released, either using imagery that involves one of the elements (light, earth, air, water, fire) or in whatever way the part chooses. After unburdening, the part can invite qualities of its own choosing to fill the space formerly occupied by the burden.

REFERENCES

Abrahms Spring, J. (2004). *How can I forgive you? The courage to forgive, the freedom not to.* New York, NY: Harper Collins.

Assagioli, R. (1975). *Psychosynthesis: A manual of principles and techniques.* London: Turnstone Press. (Original work published 1965).

Badenoch, B. (2008). *Being a brain-wise therapist, a practical guide to interpersonal neurobiology.* New York, NY: Norton.

Bowen, M. (1978). *Family therapy in clinical practice.* New York, NY: Jason Aronson.

Bowlby, J.M. (1969). *Attachment and loss: Vol. 1. Attachment.* New York, NY: Basic Books.

Bradshaw, J. (1988). *Healing the shame that binds you.* Deerfield, FL: Health Communications.

Coan, J.A., Schaefer, H.S. & Davidson, R.J. (2006) Lending a hand: Social regulation of the neural response to threat. *Psychological Science, 17,* 1032–1039.

Cozolino, L.J. (2002). *The neuroscience of psychotherapy, building and rebuilding the human brain.* New York, NY: Norton.

Cozolino, L.J. (2006). *The neuroscience of human relationships, attachment and the developing social brain.* New York, NY: Norton.

Cozolino, L.J. (2008). It's a jungle in there. *Psychotherapy Networker,* September/October, 20–27.

Ecker, B., Ticic, R. & Hulley, L. (2012). *Unlocking the emotional brain, eliminating symptoms at their roots using memory reconsolidation.* New York, NY: Routledge.

Fisher, R. (2002). *Experiential psychotherapy with couples, a guide for the creative pragmatist.* Phoenix, AZ: Zeig, Tucker and Theisen Inc.

Freud, S. (1961). The ego and the id. In J. Strachey (Ed. and Trans.), *The standard edition of the complete psychological works of Sigmund Freud* (Vol. 19, pp. 19–27). London: Hogarth Press. (Original work published 1923).

Hendrix, H. (1988). *Getting the love you want.* New York, NY: Henry Holt and Company.

Johnson, S.M. (2004). *The practice of emotionally focused couple therapy: Creating connection.* New York, NY: Brunner-Routledge.

Johnson, S.M. (2013). *Love sense: The revolutionary new science of romantic relationships.* New York, NY: Little, Brown & Co.

Jung, C.G. (1969). *The collected works of C.G. Jung (2nd ed.): Vol. 8. The structure and dynamics of the psyche* (H. Read, M. Fordham, & G. Adler, Eds.; R.F.C. Hull, Trans.). Princeton, NJ: Princeton University Press.

Kabat-Zinn, J. (1990). *Full catastrophe living: Using the wisdom of your body and mind to face stress, pain and illness.* New York, NY: Dell Publishing.

Kaufman, G. (1980). *Shame, the power of caring.* Rochester, Vermont: Schenkman Books Inc.

Lewis, H.B. (1987). *The role of shame in symptom formation.* Hillsdale, NJ: Psychology Press.

Lewis, T., Amini, F. & Lannon, R. (2000). *A general theory of love.* New York, NY: Random House.

Lind-Kyle, P. (2009). *Heal your mind, rewire your brain.* Santa Rosa, CA: Energy Psychology Press.

McCarthy, B., & McCarthy, E. (2003). *Rekindling desire, a step-by-step program to help low sex and no sex marriages.* New York, NY: Routledge.

McConnell, S. (2013). Embodying the internal family. In M. Sweezy & E. Ziskind (Eds.), *Internal family systems therapy: New dimensions.* (pp. 90–106). New York, NY: Routledge.

Michael, R., Gagnon, J., Laumann, E. & Kalota, G. (1994). *Sex in America.* Boston, MA: Little, Brown.

Minuchin, S., & Fishman, H. (1981). *Techniques of family therapy.* Cambridge, MA: Harvard University Press.

Neff, K.D. (2011). Self-compassion, self-esteem, and well-being. *Social and Personality Psychology Compass, 5,* 1–12.

Notarius, C. & Buongiorno, I. (1992). Unpublished study cited in John M. Gottman, James D. Murray, Catherine C. Swanson, Rebecca Tyson, & Kristin R. Swanson, *The mathematics of marriage: Dynamic nonlinear models.* Cambridge, MA: MIT Press, (1999), 34.

Porges, S.W. (2007). The polyvagal perspective. *Biological Psychology, 74,* 116–143.

Rogers, C. (1951). *Client-centered therapy: Its current practice, implications and theory.* London: Constable.

Schwartz, R.C. (1995). *Internal family systems therapy.* New York, NY: Guilford Press.

Schwartz, R.C. (2008). *You are the one you've been waiting for: Bringing courageous love to intimate relationships.* Oak Park, IL: Trailhead.

Schwartz R.C. (2013). The therapist–client relationship and the transformative power of self. In M. Sweezy & E. Ziskind (Eds.), *Internal family systems therapy: New dimensions* (pp. 1–23). New York, NY: Routledge.

Siegel, D.J. (2003). *Parenting from the inside out. How a deeper understanding can help you raise children who thrive.* New York, NY: Putnam.

Siegel, D.J. (2007). *The mindful brain: Reflection and attunement in the cultivation of well-being.* New York, NY: Norton.

Sweezy, M. (2013). Emotional cannibalism: Shame in action. In M. Sweezy & E. Ziskind (Eds.), *Internal family systems therapy: New dimensions* (pp. 24–34). New York, NY: Routledge.

Watkins, H.H., & Watkins, J.G. (1997). *Ego states: Theory and therapy.* New York, NY: W.W. Norton.

INDEX

8 Cs 179

abhorred parts 4
Abrahms Spring, J. 165, 169
affairs 2, 33, 92–3; case example
    159–72
aggressive parts, intervening with
    61–2
Amini, F. 136
amygdala 17–18
angry parts 127–8; validating and
    unblending 96, 97, 99–101
apology 31, 32, 157, 158, 164, 172;
    authentic 165–8, 173–4; bad
    158–9; non-acceptance of
    168–9, 171
archetypes 11
Assagioli, R. 11
attachment 53; internal 73, 74, 75,
    76, 83; secure 50, 74
attuned listening 74
attunement 2, 81, 136, 140; internal
    23; therapist 54, 132; see also
    misattunement
autonomic nervous system 4, 16, 19,
    35, 131, 138, 139, 144, 150

Badenoch, B. 75
behavior: assessing patterns of 15,
    16, 39; see also tracking; trying
    new 131; see also experiential
    work

being in flow 12
belief systems 12
blame/blaming 5, 23, 51–2, 165;
    acceptance of 158; cycle 69,
    116, 117 (interrupting
    119–29)
blending of parts 13–14, 21, 60, 151,
    162, 176–7; defined 181;
    therapist 145, 146
body language 64, 76, 121, 160
Bograd, M. 87
Bowen, M. 87
Bowlby, J.M. 11
Bradshaw, J. 129
Buddha mind 12
Buongiorno, I. 22
burdens/burdened parts 75, 182

case studies: experiential work
    (Michelle and Juliet) 133–7;
    first session and introducing
    model (Susan and Marco)
    22–4, 26, 27–30, 31–4;
    identifying negative cycles
    (Xander and Naomi) 16–17,
    18; individual work (Nadine
    and Mitch) 77–81, 82;
    negotiating needs (Tom and
    Isabel/Vera and Peter)
    97–103, 107–13; redoing
    conflict (Damien and Justine)
    138–42; repairing relationship

rupture (Ben and Jill) 159–72; sexual relationships (Susan and Marco/Elizabeth and Jonathan) 33, 64–9; shame/shaming (Alex and David) 119–29; speaking and listening (Seamus and Lori/Luke and Adrienne) 53–60, 60–3; tracking cycles (Sophie and Sam) 40–7
change, possibility of 27–8, 35, 96
childhood experiences 73, 74, 75, 76, 96, 97, 101–2, 106, 113, 114, 115
Choice in Every Moment exercise, A 103–5
clients see couples
Coan, J.A. 11
communication 4, 16, 50–72; about sexual relationships 33, 63–9; contingent 50; courageous 51–3; empathic 50; importance of 50–1
compassion 2, 4, 139, 168, 169; listening with 52; self- 93, 116, 129, 169
complexes 11
confession 165
conflict: intrapsychic 11; as never one-sided 171; as normal 157; redoing 138–42
confrontation 61, 62
connection: need for 3, 5, 39, 95, 113; Self-to-Self 4
contingent communication 50
countertransference 85–94, 146, 175
couples: concerns about therapy 25–7; early relationship 28–9; getting to know 21–35; goals and wishes 27–8; introducing concepts of IFIO to 29–31
Cozolino, L.J. 18, 136, 139
curiosity 2, 133; listening with 52, 53

de-centering 14
de-shaming 4, 5

depolarization 5
differences, toleration of 5, 6
differentiation 15, 16, 29, 52, 53, 70, 73, 115
difficult cases 145–53
direct access 46, 61, 130, 181–2
disappointment, toleration of 5
disgraced parts 4
dissociation 124

early relationship of couples 28–9
Ecker, B. 20, 81
ego 11
ego state therapy 11
emotional needs see needs
emotional synchrony, client–therapist 88–9
emotions 2, 47; and action 47; regulation of 47; and the Self 2
empathy 50, 54, 71, 72, 73, 77, 145, 165
ending sessions 34
exiles see vulnerable parts
experiential work 131–44; feeling closer 133–8; how to do 143–4; redoing conflict 138–42; and unblending of parts 131, 133, 138–9, 143
eye contact 42, 43, 74, 76, 82

family of origin 32
fear 95, 133
Feldman, K. and Feldman, J. 103
fight (or collapse) cycle 96, 97, 99
fight-or-flight response 79, 119, 140
firefighters (protective parts) 13, 180, 181
Fisher, R. 132, 143
Fishman, H. 18, 39
focusing on one partner 42–3
forgiveness 6, 157, 158, 159, 167, 168–71, 172, 174; refusing to forgive 169, 174; self- 157, 159, 164–5, 173

Freud, S. 11
frustrated parts, validation and
      unblending of 96, 97, 99–101

Gagnon, J. 68
Geib, P. 145
gender roles 66–8
going forward 6

Hakomi 132
healing, intrapersonal and
      interpersonal 15–16
Hendrix, H. 52–3, 132
hope 27–8
hopelessness 23, 27, 28
humiliated parts 170
humor 41, 133

id 11
Imago dialogue 52–3, 132
implicit memory 18, 19, 74
individual work 4, 73–84; partner as
      witness in 75, 76, 77, 82, 83
infidelity 92–3; see also affairs
inner child approaches 11
inner light 12
internal attachment 73, 74, 75, 76, 83
Internal Family Systems Therapy
      (IFS) 1, 11, 13, 14, 15
interpersonal healing 15–16
Intimacy from the Inside Out
      (IFIO) 1; blueprint for 2–3;
      three phases of treatment 3–7
intrapersonal healing 15–16

Johnson, S.M. 11, 74
judging part 141
judgmentalism 23
Jung, C.G. 11

Kabat-Zinn, J. 14
Kalota, G. 68
Kaufman, G. 117, 128, 129, 151

Lannon, R. 136

Laumann, E. 68
Lewis, H.B. 117
Lewis, T. 136, 140, 144
limbic resonance 136–7, 140, 144
Lind-Kyle, P. 96, 132
listening 22, 23, 53–63, 70, 71, 72;
      attuned 74; with compassion
      52; with curiosity 52, 53; from
      the Self 4, 52, 82, 161–4, 166,
      173, 175; mindful 56, 57
loneliness 95
longing 95
love 136; need for 3, 5, 39, 95

McCarthy Model of sexual therapy
      69
McConnell, S. 87
managers (protective parts) 13, 41,
      180–1
mapping parts 49
memory, implicit 18, 19, 74
Michael, R. 68
mindful listening and speaking 56,
      57
mindfulness 14, 93
Minuchin, S. 18, 39
mirroring 22, 35, 53, 74
misattunement 74, 95, 157

needs 18, 141–2; conflicting and
      corresponding needs 5,
      106–15; for connection 3, 5,
      39, 95, 113; for love 3, 5, 39,
      95; for safety 3, 22, 39, 114–5;
      negotiation of 5, 95–105; true
      95–6; unmet 3–4, 39
Neff, K.D. 93, 94, 129
negative cycles: between client and
      therapist 148–50; identifying
      16–19; tracking 3–4, 39–48
non-demand pleasure 69
normalizing 22, 114
Notarius, C. 22

parasympathetic nervous system 35
parts 2, 11–13, 180; abhorred 4;

aggressive 61–2; and belief systems 12; burdened 75, 182; detector, therapist as 4, 21, 70; disgraced 4; emerging 131–2; humiliated 170; introducing concept to couples 29–30; judging 141; and Self relationship 5–6, 13, 15, 19, 47, 74, 75, 106, 164, 172, 176; speaking for 53–4, 60–2, 70, 71, 72, 96, 161–4, 166, 173, 175; target 79, 181; therapist 23, 130, 132, 145, 146, 147, 149–50, 151–2, 153, 166; of the therapist 146, 147; *see also* angry parts; blending of parts; frustrated parts; protective parts; unblending of parts; unburdening; vulnerable parts

polarization 5, 114, 181

polyvagal theory 137, 139–40

Porges, S.W. 22, 79, 137, 139–40, 141, 144

possibility of change 27–8, 35, 96

predictable/unpredictable dialectic 2–3

preparedness 2

protective parts 2–3, 11–12, 13, 14, 16, 18, 44–7, 55, 90, 151; defined 180–1; firefighters 13, 180, 181; managers 13, 41, 180–1; in relationship 19; therapist 147; unblending of 96, 97, 129, 131, 138–9, 162

questions, initial 25

rage 2, 117

re-turn 52, 70, 75, 96, 97, 103

reaching out 74

reconciliation 6

redoing conflict 138–42

reflecting back 22, 23, 43, 48

relational triangle 87–8

relational unburdening 4, 16, 20, 75, 81, 178

remorse 165

repair 6, 16, 157–75; as crucial 158–9; how to (step 1: creating safety 160–1, 173; step 2: speaking and listening 161–4, 173; step 3: self-inquiry and self-forgiveness 164–5, 173; step 4: authentic apology 165–8, 173–4; step 5: setting an intention 168, 174; step 6: forgiveness 168–71, 174; step 7: shared responsibility 171–2, 175)

requests, making 16, 96, 100, 103, 113, 114

resonance, limbic 136–7, 140, 144

responsibility: shared 171–2, 175; taking 168

Rogers, C. 72, 88

sadness 95, 133

safety 14, 76, 82, 83, 138, 162; creating 26, 35, 137, 160–1, 173; needs 3, 22, 39, 124–5

Schwartz, R.C. 1, 2, 3, 4, 11, 12, 13, 19, 21, 39, 46, 53, 58, 60, 74, 93, 106, 113, 151, 168, 178

secrets 35

secure attachment 50

secure internal attachment 74, 75

Self 2, 12, 57, 106, 176, 177, 179; introducing concept to couples 30–1; listening from 4, 52, 82, 161–4, 166, 173, 175; qualities of: The 8 Cs 179

self-care 105

self-compassion 93, 94, 116, 129, 169

self-disclosure 52

Self-energy 30, 47, 63, 73, 74, 83, 91, 103, 115, 129, 143, 165, 166, 175

self-forgiveness 157, 159, 164–5, 173
self-identity 12
self-inquiry 164–5, 173
self-knowledge 116
Self-leadership 3, 14, 33, 35, 93, 104, 139, 180
self-regulation 5; therapist 145, 150
Self-to-parts relationship 5–6, 13, 15, 19, 47, 74, 75, 106, 164, 172
Self-to-Self connection 4
self-worth 165–6
sexual relationships:
    communicating about 33, 63–9; non-demand pleasure in 69
shame/shaming 2–3, 5, 11, 51–2, 90, 95, 115, 116–30, 157, 164–5, 172; cycle 69, 116, 117; interrupting 119–29; effect on intimate relationships 118; exiles 118; healing shame 118–19; protectors 56, 116, 117, 118, 128–9, 130, 176; recognizing 129–30; therapist 151–2; therapist's role in working with 117; unburdening 16, 19, 83
Siegel, D.J. 18, 50, 59, 72, 95, 116
soul 12
speaking: mindful 56, 57; for parts 53–4, 60–2, 70, 71, 72, 96, 161–4, 166, 173, 175
stressors, normal 32–3
sub-personalities 11
superego 11
Sweezy, M. 117, 128
sympathetic nervous system 35

Tao 12
target part 79, 181
tender touch 74
therapist: attunement 54, 132; blending of parts 145, 146; countertransference 85–94,
146, 175; embodied 86–7; emotional synchrony with client 88–9; empathy 54, 71, 72; initial questions 25; inner critic 90–1; negative cycle between client and 148–50; parts 23, 130, 132, 145, 146, 147, 149–50, 151–2, 153, 166; as parts detector 4, 21, 70; parts of the 146, 147; patience and persistence 60; protective parts 147; role of 21; self-regulation 145, 150; shaming and shamed parts 151–2; triangulated 87; U-turn 85–6, 93, 147, 149; unblending of parts 58, 147, 150, 153; vulnerable part 147
tracking 3–4, 175; cycles 3–4, 39–48, 70
triangles, relational 87–8

U-turn 19, 40, 48, 52, 60, 70, 73, 75, 79, 96, 97, 130, 164, 174; therapist 85–6, 93, 147, 149
unblending of parts 3–4, 5, 14, 15, 16, 19, 29, 47, 52, 56, 71, 113–14, 151, 175, 176–7; anger 96, 97, 129; as counterintuitive 162; defined 181; and experiential work 131, 133, 138–9, 143; frustration 96, 97; techniques 49; therapist 58, 147, 150, 153; using direct access 130
unburdening 5, 16, 74–5, 177–8; defined 182; relational 4, 16, 20, 75, 81, 178; of shame 16, 19, 83

validating 22, 53, 54, 61, 62, 130, 162; angry part 96, 97, 99–101; frustrated part 96, 97, 99–101; vulnerable part 98
ventral vagus nerve 137, 139–40

visuals, to promote unblending 49
vulnerability 18
vulnerable parts (exiles) 4, 13, 14,
      16, 20, 39, 45, 71, 74, 138–9;
      defined 180; encouraging
      expression of 135–6, 138; and
      the Self 12; therapist 147;
unburdening of, in individual
      work 76; validating 98

Watkins, H.H. and Watkins, J.G. 11
witnessing 73, 182; internal 129; of
      partners, in individual work
      75, 76, 77, 82, 83

Made in the USA
Coppell, TX
29 March 2022